D1242137

GROWING STRONGER

GROWING STRONGER

THALIA

A CELEBRA BOOK

CELEBRA
Published by New American Library,
a division of Penguin Group (USA) Inc.,
375 Hudson Street, New York, New York 10014, USA
Penguin Group (Canada), 90 Eglinton Avenue East, Suite 700, Toronto,
Ontario M4P 2Y3, Canada (a division of Pearson Penguin Canada Inc.)
Penguin Books Ltd., 80 Strand, London WC2R 0RL, England
Penguin Ireland, 25 St. Stephen's Green, Dublin 2,
Ireland (a division of Penguin Books Ltd.)
Penguin Group (Australia), 250 Camberwell Road, Camberwell, Victoria 3124,
Australia (a division of Pearson Australia Group Pty. Ltd.)
Penguin Books India Pvt. Ltd., 11 Community Centre, Panchsheel Park,
New Delhi - 110 017, India
Penguin Group (NZ), 67 Apollo Drive, Rosedale, Auckland 0632,
New Zealand (a division of Pearson New Zealand Ltd.)
Penguin Books (South Africa) (Pty.) Ltd., 24 Sturdee Avenue,
Rosebank, Johannesburg 2196, South Africa

Penguin Books Ltd., Registered Offices:
80 Strand, London WC2R 0RL, England

Published by Celebra, an imprint of New American Library,
a division of Penguin Group (USA) Inc.

First Printing, November 2011
10   9   8   7   6   5   4   3   2   1

Copyright © Lady Thalia, LLC, 2011
Translated by Monica Haim
All rights reserved

CELEBRA and logo are trademarks of Penguin Group (USA) Inc.

LIBRARY OF CONGRESS CATALOGING-IN-PUBLICATION DATA:
Thalia.
Growing stronger / Thalia.
p.   cm.
ISBN 978-0-451-23441-4
1. Thalia.   2. Singers—Mexico—Biography.   3. Actors—Mexico—Biography.
ML420.T3938A3   2011
782.42164092—dc23
[B]   2011031503

Set in Fairfield LT STD
Designed by Elke Sigal

Printed in the United States of America

*For Sabrina, who fuels me with the urge to seek
an even better version of myself every single day.*

*For Matthew, whose presence reminds me that
life is filled with miracles and hidden treasures.*

*For Tommy, who has held my hand throughout an
extraordinary journey full of passion, and who has shown
me the true meaning of the word* commitment.

*For my mother, whose gaze alone transmitted unconditional
love, a love that has transcended the grave.
You will always be in my heart, in every place and thought
we ever shared, forever and ever.*

My fans and followers, especially if they are young like me, in every circumstance of their lives feel as though they are someone wearing clothing that isn't their size.

(. . .)

When I have felt down, it was due to a méprise, *a misunderstanding with regard to personality; I have, in effect, considered myself to be someone that I am not, and I have lamented his disgrace; think of myself, for example, a* Privatdozent, *who is unable to obtain a professorship or a no from students; or somehow who is censored by this hypocrite, or criticized by that grand society dame; or like the convict on trial for defamation; or like the lover who does not correspond with the young girl who so infatuated him; or like the patient convalescing in his house; or like any other person who ruminates on these types of miseries: I have been none of these; it has been about something other than me, a piece of cloth that perhaps has been cut from something that I wore for a while, but which I later threw out and replaced with another.*

So, who am I?

—ARTHUR SCHOPENHAUER,
The Art of Knowing One's Self

GROWING STRONGER

· PRELUDE ·

G*rowing Stronger* emerged from a need to relate my life experiences as well as my constant struggle to prevail each day, and as a reminder to myself of the importance of never giving up. There are moments that are decisive and transcendental, which have in some way impacted me deeply, a path that I had to chart, no matter how or where I was. The important thing was the desire and decision to do so—to conquer it, to walk it, to experience it, take it in, and most of all, to live it fully.

As I wrote this book, I also lived through two critical and transformative events: my second pregnancy, the announcement of a new life that I will soon hold in my arms, inviting joy to knock on my door once again; and the death of my beloved mother, Yolanda, the single most important person in my life, whose total devotion, support, direction, excellent counsel and unconditional love armed me with the tools to face this moment of joy that came with the arrival of our family's newest member, but also the total devastation of her sudden loss.

I started the book during a time when I felt that I had found myself, existing on a plane of optimal and harmonious balance regarding my thoughts and feelings alike, having made peace with my past—and I finished the book with a sense of fullness and liberation that I, in turn, wanted to share with you.

But God had other plans, and because the book was already in production, I decided to include and share the latest of my great tests—the irreparable loss of my mother, who is the most cherished person in my life.

One week prior to her death, my mother—such the enthusiast about everything—held this finalized manuscript, which she not only read twice, but also edited, adding her comments where necessary and making revisions that we instantly addressed in the book.

Since I was a little girl, I have witnessed the strength and courage that energized my mother, who left every sorrow and pain in the past, who would work unyieldingly to obtain her goals, who was the great warrior from whom I learned all the values that are today fundamental pillars of my every day.

She raised me to have a steady character; she held my hand, and with her I discovered an infinite world of possibilities and dreams that could become a reality. Her essence came through in all of my stories, in my daily life, in my dreams and desires. My mother shared all of it, always full of life and passion, as only she could be, one with freedom, shining like the sun and eating up the blessings and opportunities of life by hungry mouthfuls.

My mother was a little girl who never grew up, and sometimes we would laugh, and I would say things like, "Okay, so now it looks like I am your mother and you are my daughter," to which she would reply, "Well, yes. Handle it and pamper me." I wish this could really be true with the birth of my baby: that somehow her spirit could be born again in this new creature who will fill my house with love, that I could have her in my arms and cuddle her with so much love close to my heart. But I know that she was called by God to follow the path that He has for her.

My mother's impetuous personality and her limitless way of being touched so many of the people who knew her. She filled some of them with love, with optimism, with faith and smiles. To others she imparted wise advice during their difficult times, helping them along; and she transformed others into great impresarios, talented businessmen, professionals with the capacity to develop in any field; likewise with her closest people, such as her family, friends, acquaintances and colleagues, from her banker to her hairdresser. All of them always felt a lot of love for her and felt loved by her, a gift that very few people have.

This book is a celebration of love and joy, an homage that through the course of my life experiences, most of it accompanied by her, I want to share with you, my readers.

In *Growing Stronger*, I expose my most painful moments and open my heart, thoughts and person, so that my experiences can inspire alleviation, consolation and decisiveness.

Like everyone else, there are things that motivate me, as well as things that detract and paralyze me. With this book, which is filled with a sentiment of fortitude and potential, I want to inspire people to live their lives fully, for us to always see a light along the way, and in this way be able to embrace, forgive, restore and love.

Through my remembrances, past and present, I discovered the power that I carry within, much of which I inherited directly from my mother.

I realized that every experience, every hardship, problem, painful ordeal, difficult or intense, has allowed me to know myself better each time. I hope with all my heart that through my experiences and story you will be able to find that sense of motivation that, as it did for me, will inspire you to discover the marvelous person that you are, even in the midst of storminess and pain. This book reflects the trajectory of my life, which I hope will help you along your path and in your search. If this book helps you at all with your own life, that will be the greatest gift for me.

Thank you, Mother, because you taught me to be stronger every day.

—*Thalia*

· CHAPTER ONE ·

CHILDHOOD

D*ear Llorona:*

I am writing this letter to thank you for everything that you have done for me, which of course I had to grow up to really understand.

I don't know if you remember how we met: My mother was pregnant with me the first time we saw you. It was a warm night, and my father had gone to another room, leaving her alone in the bedroom to rest; she was sleeping peacefully when she suddenly heard your voice—your wails, rather. You were standing right there, right next to her. You wore a black hat and a long dress. Your hands were long and bony, both of which you used to cover your face, but that still somehow allowed your cries to escape, along with your weeping laments that shattered the silence of the night. Your tangled hair gave you a spectral aspect and my mother barely dared to look at you. With eyes

half-open in the midst of the darkness, she tried to look
for my father, reaching her foot out to him, desperately
seeking his help. She was terrified and practically
immobilized from the great pang of dread that had
overtaken her. And I believe that somehow or other, while
I was nestled inside her womb, I also sought the protection
of my father. When she didn't find him next to her, she
slowly built up her courage, and, taking two steps at a
time, she ran to the room where he had gone to sleep
because the heat generated by my mother's body in her
advanced state of pregnancy was unbearable; I was just a
few weeks away from being born. She fled quickly, feeling
the reach of your hands upon her back, with a fear so
intense that she slipped herself beneath my father, under
his virile body, utterly terrorized. Her horror-struck eyes
were wide-open, and she was totally unable to speak.
He told her to breathe deeply, and managed to calm
my mother down, which is when she stopped hearing
your cries.

But nobody silences La Llorona. This was proven to me
when we met again a few years later in that spacious and
empty house—the very one that you are so well acquainted
with. Who knows, perhaps it was your own home many
years ago. But this time I was alone. I went downstairs to
pour myself a glass of water and there you were. I'll never
know for sure whether it was in fact you, because you
covered your face with those cadaverous hands of yours—
the hands that remained forever etched in my mother's
mind, but my intuition and the visceral impression that
I had experienced from my mother's womb somehow
confirmed your presence. A black veil shrouded your face

and you wept inconsolably. It was more like a wolf howling wildly deep into the night. I was just four years old. Now that I think about it, I never had imaginary friends, because chances are that they, too, would have been terrified of you.

Luckily, I don't hear you anymore. . . . For now I will say farewell to you, thanking you for teaching me that fears are like phantoms: When you detect them, you must confront and dissipate them, powerfully moving forward with your head held high, proud of what you have accomplished. Ever since, I have learned to overcome.

I no longer fear you, Llorona.

Silence

I was just starting to learn how to speak my thoughts fully when I was all of a sudden left speechless. I was only six years old when my father passed away, and my pain was so severe that silence became my only option.

My father was Ernesto Sodi Pallares. He suffered from advanced diabetes, but when he was diagnosed, he decided to continue living without any modifications or restrictions, relishing his favorite dishes, fine wines, and spirits, a genuine epicurean. But by making that decision, he pretty much signed his own death certificate. The impact of his loss was so great for me that I decided not to talk; for one whole year I opted only for silence. I don't remember exactly what I was thinking, but I knew that I could not emit even one sound, because whatever came out of my mouth would be too painful. I would ask myself where my partner in games had disappeared to, he who had shown me so many amazing things in his chemistry lab, the generous father who taught me how to play with all of his obscure scientific equipment. Where was he? Never again would I hear his voice calling my name, laughing, telling me a story or reading me a poem. Never again would I see him or touch him; I would never again fall asleep in his arms . . . never.

Concerned about my unsettling silence and intense sorrow, my mother consulted with various doctors to try to understand what was happening to me. Some even thought it was autism. We went to see numerous specialists, visited countless doctors' offices, took endless exams, all of which created in me such a profound fascination with psychology that I continue to study it to this day. I loved visiting all those doctors, some of whom even showed me those famous black inkblots, and in turn analyzed what I drew to express what I had seen in the markings.

After a series of long days spent in hospitals and therapists' offices and enduring exhaustive analyses, I was diagnosed as suffering from deep shock due to my father's death. The doctors explained to my mother that everything appeared to be normal physically, and told her to be very patient and loving with me so that I could overcome my father's absence. They determined that I didn't speak because I didn't want to speak, and they assured her that I would talk again as soon as I snapped out of this mighty state of shock; I simply had to find my way back, face reality, find resolution within and accept what had happened. But how do you teach a very young child how to release pain? How do you show her? To that end, the whole strategy at home changed, and instead of adding to the trauma by asking me too many questions, they held on to the hope that this great silence would one day break.

And that is exactly what happened. When I was finally ready, one day I began to speak. We were seated at the dining room table when suddenly I said to my mother: "Where is my father?" Trying to contain her enormous surprise and joy in hearing me speak, with the sweetest tone in her voice she explained to me that he was no longer with us, that he had passed away—just like some of the animals I had kept as pets had passed away—but that he was okay, and now lived in heaven. I listened to her words, which helped me to begin healing that massive pain I carried within. Most important, I started to talk again. My life continued as normal—as normal as can be for a six-year-old girl under such circumstances, because at the center of it was a challenging period of healing, introspection, mourning and deep sadness.

Prior to his illness, my relationship with my father was very strong. He had this lovely, poetic way of speaking when he communicated with me. It was as if he spoke in verse at all times; he would always recite poetry to me, and that was just how we conversed. He would tell me, for example, that blood is the life force of the body, and he would go on to talk about the various cases that he was working on in his job as a criminologist. We would spend entire afternoons looking at little orbs under the lens of a microscope, which were nothing more than blood cells. My father taught me how to be visual, to always seek the details in everything and to pay attention to the simplest things, those that often seem irrelevant to others. He is the one who taught me how to be curious and inquisitive. He was a loving, sweet and dedicated father to me. But my sisters don't remember him as I do, because they had to deal with a man who was strong in character, seemingly invincible and totally inflexible. My mother had to contend with a possessive, demanding perfectionist. But the father that I remember was already sick, physically weak and a lot more humbled, because life had presented him with an unexpected twist that deeply affected his ego. Because of his illness, he became dependent on those around him; he who had always been so radically independent, who never needed anyone, was now subject to the availability of others. For me he always was and will always be a complete and total man, the greatest scientist and one of my best friends.

The day my father died, I was taken to the hospital to see him. Before that, when he was still at home, he spent his last days lying in bed. The pungent smell of medicine and sickness had become a part of our household and our everyday lives. I would enter his room as always, with the childhood confidence that could never fathom rejection, and I would climb onto his bed, where we would fall deeply into conversation. He would ask me to turn on the television and then he would explain the plots of the shows we were watching. He would always cuddle me with his big, fatherly hands, and I would lie there next to him, cozily nestled under his arm. One day, however, I did not see him in his bed, and when I asked where my father was, I was told that he had gone to the hospital: "He is sick and doesn't feel well," my family would say over and over again. But I wanted to see him; I longed to see him, to chat with my partner in games, fairy tales, and wonderful and unforgettable stories; I yearned for his company; I missed his smell; I needed to fall into his arms and feel loved, secure and happy. However, deep inside my heart, I knew that something serious had happened. The events of those last days planted a scene in my memory that I did not understand until much later in my life. The very same day that my father was taken to the emergency room, I was left in the care of one of my sisters, and when I went into his room I saw in his bathroom, which had a white wooden floor and walls covered with black and white tiles, that the housekeeper was cleaning the fresh blood that had splattered onto the walls and left a vivid trail of red from the sink to the toilet.

When my mother finally took me to the hospital to see him, I was shocked to find him unconscious, connected to so many machines, intubated with lines and surrounded by IVs and blood bags. The doctors were desperately trying to give him even the smallest breath of life. I didn't know that he was in a coma; I just thought that he was deep in sleep. So at one point, my mother quietly said, "Go over to him and get close to his ear and slowly tell him that you love him very much." I made my way toward him with great caution and told him that I loved him, and said goodbye to him with a kiss. We left the room almost immediately, and the moment we crossed the threshold of the doorway, the sounds of the machines all started to go off, the nurses rushed in and the doctors were called.

My father was dying.

At the time, I somehow felt that my father had died because I gave him a kiss. That belief is how my silence began. Even when I finally started to speak again and it seemed like I was regaining some sense of normalcy, the memory of that kiss was etched into every little fiber of my being: a kiss of love that provoked death, a traumatic moment that I will likely carry inside for many more years of my life.

My Childhood

I was born eleven years after my sister Ernestina, and totally by accident. I say it was an accident because after such a long time, my parents were not thinking about having any more children, so I arrived unannounced, by total surprise, and with no type of warning. I am the youngest of five girls.

I grew up in Mexico City, in a neighborhood that was called Santa María la Ribera, which was constructed in the early 1900s by the acting president of the Mexican Republic, Porfirio Díaz, as an exclusive enclave for the upper echelons of society. As such, you can find the first theater erected by the Porfiriato (the government of Porfirio Díaz); the great courthouse, which is currently the Geology Museum; and the renowned museum of El Chopo, which housed all sorts of collections—archaeological, ethnographic, paleontological, mineral, biological and beyond—that were relocated to other museums in the capital as the years went by. There was a section in that museum of tiny little fleas all dressed up that was my favorite, and which all the children would compete to see through a large magnifying glass that hung over the boxes containing the fleas.

When my father built the house for my mother, the district was no longer considered that important, because many of the families had moved to Polanco, Chapultepec and Reforma. By the time I was born, the neighborhood's economy was on the decline, but I remember it as a lovely area. Somehow or other, it retained the air of importance that suggested the former presence of significant Mexican personalities, such as La Prieta Linda, who sang folk songs that are more commonly known as *rancheras*, accompanied by a band of mariachis; or Dr. Atl, the great Mexican painter who depicted the vibrant Mexican landscapes in his work. To this day, the streets honor the most significant Mexican thinkers, historians and poets of the time, such as Alzate, Amado Nervo and Díaz Mirón. It felt like an unparalleled privilege to hear my father, who was uniquely gifted with a sharp memory, reciting the poems of each of these great men, or telling us their stories as we walked down one of the streets that were named after them.

One of the main streets of my neighborhood was San Cosme, a wide road with a median down the middle. On the weekends I would ask my mother if we could go *sancosm-ing*, because the San

Cosme market was near our house and we liked to browse and shop around there. We would get to the museum of El Chopo, which always featured very interesting exhibitions, beautiful art, sculpture and poetry classes for children. Later we would eat at a small restaurant that is still open today called La Tonina, where they serve the best *caldillo de queso* (a chicken-based broth with melted cheese) and fresh flour tortillas that I have ever tasted. According to my sister Federica, they are still as delicious to this very day. The owner was Tonina Jackson, the famous Mexican wrestler from the fifties. On one side of the street was the Teatro Virginia Fábregas, and on the other side, just a few feet away, the Cine Opera, where we would watch double features: two films for the price of one. In that theater, along with the popcorn, my cherished *gaznates* awaited me, a type of candy that you can find anywhere in Mexico, but which was originally made by the nuns who many years ago lived in Puebla, just two hours away from the capital. Today, many people make this treat, which is a very delicate wafer filled with a meringue made of honey and a few drops of lemon. It's the kind of taste that sends you straight to cloud nine, and, of course, I always had to accompany it with my favorite orange soda.

By the time we left the theater, the market stalls would already be assembled and filled with all sorts of trinkets and goodies that could never be found in any Mexican store. These kiosks sold things that, at the time, were available only in the United States, such as blow-dryers, jackets, Nike sneakers, Walkmans, makeup, and an array of countless amazing oddities that would take me an eternity to list. Week after week we would go back to that colorful market to see what new things had arrived. Chances are it was all contraband.

Being there was overwhelming, with streets upon streets of

little stands the color of *rosa mexicano*, that typically Mexican bright pink hue that was used and popularized by Diego Rivera and Frida Kahlo. The little stands were all lined with a string of lightbulbs so that everyone could see what was in each one. When you walked past a stand, the salesperson would usually scream to get your attention: "Cooooommmmeee onnnn throooogh, come on through. . . . We are selling three for the price of one; browse without obligation; if you don't like it, we'll gladly exchange it. Come on through." I would walk through the aisles of stands eating one of the local hotcakes, which were plump and doughy, and had a type of caramel that we called *cajeta*—similar to *dulce de leche*—all wrapped in a piece of brown paper with grease. Just thinking about it makes my mouth water. Absolutely delicious.

My people, my language, the melodies of everyday life in Mexico are songs from the neighborhood that now sound glorious in my memory. That's how my childhood was, rich with culture and vibrant with wonderful colors and smells.

La Calle Díaz Mirón

Legend has it that there was a cemetery beneath our house and around the corner there was a church. In more opulent times, it is said that the more privileged families built secret tunnels to access said church so that they wouldn't have to mingle with the common folk. When he renovated our house, my father sealed off the tunnel that connected our home to the church. I've always been curious about what could possibly lie within those tunnels: obscure treasures or gold coins hidden in the walls . . . but to this day I still do not know.

At the end of the fifties my father inherited a house in Santa María, on Calle Díaz Mirón, on the corner of Sabino, which he ultimately tore down in order to build the house that we lived in when I was growing up. Originally, our house had two floors, but years later he would add a third floor that he used as his laboratory. The facade of this house features forty-two stone sculptures of dogs called *xolotl tepetlxcuincles,* which in the Nahuatl language means "small stone dog." Some of them are posing on their hind legs, while others are lying down with their heads upright. It was thanks to this collection of sculptures that the house was aptly christened "the House of the Dogs." The house also boasts four cannons like the ones used in ancient wars, stamped with the words *Calle Díaz Mirón* in iron, which function as drains for the roof; a decorative band of talavera (handmade artisan pottery from Puebla) dishes encrusted along the facade; and an iron sculpture of a head representing one of the child heroes who, according to national history, was famous for defending Chapultepec Castle. The artist who gave my father this head—which served as the model for the sculptures that actually adorn one of the balconies of that beautiful castle—was Abel Quezada, my sister Gabriela's godfather.

In fact, the house is as much an archaeological point of reference as it is a historic one, and some of my fans have made an adventure out of going there to snap a photo in front of my childhood home. Through the advent of social networks, hundreds of them have sent me pictures of themselves in front of the old house, which is deeply gratifying to me. In 2000, my mother had the house renovated and put it up for sale, and funnily enough, the buyers ended up being my old neighbors, whom my family referred to as "the little nuns from next door," the very ones who prepared me for my first communion. Today it is a part of their home and convent.

My Father

We lived on the first two floors, and the third floor was left exclusively for my father; this was where he kept his forensics and chemistry lab, and where you could see all sorts of strange instruments and criminal investigations that were under way. Some of the most unusual objects included a collection of human heads reduced to the size of grapefruits, which was a tradition of the indigenous Shuar tribe. It was as strange as it sounds. My father always adored odd and decadent images. He showed his collection to me with such great passion that I learned to appreciate them as objects of art. He was so obsessed with those heads that he actually visited one of the tribes just so that he could learn about the complicated process they used to shrink the heads, using medicinal plants. Their lips and eyes were sewn shut to keep the filling made of sand, hot stones, and mixed herbs from spilling out during the shrinking process. It always amazed me that despite being shrunken, they still retained the proportions of a normal face, not to mention the fact that the hair remained the same length it had been (on some of the heads, you could still see fossilized lice eggs!).

When President Gustavo Díaz Ordaz, who governed Mexico from 1964 to 1970, was preparing to leave office, he chose my father to interview him about his government. My father's questions were by no means simple—he asked the president, for example, about the Tlatelolco genocide of 1968—but he also knew how to throw in a couple more positive ones to balance the exchange. When the interview was over, my father presented the president with a pair of cuff links made of shrunken horse heads that he had developed in his lab especially for the occasion. Ever grateful, the president immediately named my father "official commentator of Mexico," a title that he received as praise for his extensive knowledge of the nuances and traditions of every culture and state that formed the Mexican Republic.

When I recall those little heads with their mouths and eyes sewn shut, I remember that they really were rather disturbing. Now that I think about it, I wonder whether my father was subconsciously preparing me for the fame that awaited me, because sadly, my ego did in fact get the best of me on more than one occasion, so that I arrived at a point where I had to have my head "shrunk," which in Spanish would be the equivalent of having my ego deflated. But also very clear to me are the times when others attempted to shrink my soul and somehow minimize my desire and motivation to make my dreams come true.

Back then, I was only three or four years old and didn't really understand my father's tastes, but my innocence allowed me to simply enjoy our life together, be it about shrunken heads with long hair or relishing some of that chewy milk candy that we loved so much. We developed a completely unusual manner for a father and daughter to communicate, and to this day, I have never seen anything like it.

My father graduated at the age of nineteen as a chemical and pharmacological biologist, but he specialized in criminology and forensics and became an expert graphologist. Because he worked for the Mexican government and the president, he always needed to be abreast of all kinds of news, so in his office, there was a table designated solely for the placement of the day's newspapers, along with the records and files of whatever cases he was working on. One of them marked me for life: the case of the *tamalera* (maker of tamales). Large black-and-white photos showed a metal cauldron on a base lit with coal that served to keep the tamales hot. In the pot you could see the horrifying image of a man's swollen and decapitated head, boiling away along with the tamales.

The history of the case consisted of an oppressed wife who sold tamales in the market, and who, in a moment of clarity, could no longer endure the insults, blows and abuse of her alcoholic husband. So she killed him in order to make tamales out of him— tamales that she later sold from her little stand at the market. Beneath each of those bundles that were filled with the dead man's flesh was the most overwhelming proof of the murder: the man's head. The case was widely followed by the media, and my father worked on it as well. For me it was completely normal to share this and other such stories with my friends at school. I would do what my father did with me: explain things to them as a teacher would to a group of students.

As the years went by, and as I had a chance to reflect on the time that I was able to live with him, I now realize that I would have loved to know every single one of his interesting and dynamic facets. Today, the memories flush my mind with tremendous nostalgia: I understand that I was lucky enough to have a father who was out of the ordinary, a man with an amazing mind, both profound and enigmatic, an accomplished scientist, an all-around extraordinary human being. Among his many contributions to science was the discovery of *aztequina*, the very drug used by Stalin's doctor to help prolong the man's life. He worked for the government as a consultant on scientific topics. Among the most cherished of my family's possessions is his complete study of the sacred mantle of the Virgin of Guadalupe, worshiped by all Mexicans and millions of Catholics worldwide, which is found in Tepeyac, inside the church of Guadalupe in Mexico City. My father held it in his hands and scientifically analyzed every microfiber of the fabric by order of the Vatican. His discovery dropped a lot of jaws, because the fibers, he learned, were alive, a theory that he developed with his colleague Roberto Palacios Bermúdez in their 1976 publication, *Discovery of a Human Bust in the Eyes of the Virgin of Guadalupe*. From an early age, at nineteen, my father was given the title of teacher and metallurgist by the National University of Mexico; Fordham University in New York awarded him certificates in organic analysis, colloids and advanced organic synthesis; Harvard University named him professor honoris causa in the study of organic chemical structures; the National Association of Identification in Havana, Cuba, gave him the title of expert in political science; the Office of Questioned Documents in Washington, D.C., certified him as an expert in document examination; the National Bureau of Document Examiners named him an active member; the School of Criminology and Political Science of the Mexican Republic gave him the prestigious academic title of doctor of criminology ad eundem; the Bureau of Criminal Identification and Investigation gave him the title of professor emeritus of criminology; he was a professor of criminology at the American Police Academy in Washington, D.C.; he gave a series of lectures at Harvard; and the Encyclopaedia Britannica dedicated a whole page to him in one of their editions.

If my childhood was complicated, my father's was even more so: My grandfather Demetrio Sodi Guergue was a prominent lawyer in Mexico, and one of his most notorious cases was the defense of José de León Toral, the man who assassinated General Obregón (the president elect at the time), who was nicknamed "El Manco" because he was missing his right arm. León Toral talked his way in to a dinner held for Obregón by convincing the members that he was a gifted caricaturist. The gathering took place at a restaurant called La Bombilla, which was located in

San Ángel, a district found at the southern end of the city. When Toral was close enough to the general, he drew his gun and shot the president elect several times, killing him instantly.

My grandfather was chosen by the state to defend Toral, and his thesis was quite interesting: that the findings of Obregón's autopsy were inconclusive, showing that there were various types of bullets with dissimilar trajectories. In fact, as I understand it, the Mexican historian Antonio Rius Facius revisited the autopsy report, in particular the medical section, which apparently confirmed the thesis that my grandfather had presented. My father later told my sisters that the "Obregonians" would meet outside his house and yell, "Die, Sodi! Death to the defender of Toral!" My father was only ten years old at the time, but he remembered it all with impressive clarity.

My father was the last of seven living brothers; he had others who had passed away when they were very young. His upbringing was exceedingly strict, demanding solid performance and an unyielding sense of competitiveness. He was raised within a quintessential upper-class family of the time, which prized values and education far above any sentimentality. This, in turn, made him a serious man regarding various other aspects of his life. My relationship with my father was definitely a reflection of that which he lacked during his own childhood, one that was a lot more educational than warm. Today I realize that the central point of our connection was the boy that lived within him, the boy who actually never had a childhood.

The Addams Family Home

My father's persona was formed through a sense of culture that one might call eccentric, with a range of fascinating quirks and characteristics, all of which were manifest in the decor of our home. It could have been compared to the Addams family home, not because my family was ever as extravagant as the Addams clan, but because there was nothing inside the house that fit any one particular style. The walls were made of rose-colored stone that at some point my father chose to paint in a dark, coffeelike hue. His diplomas hung on the walls, along with an impressive collection of miniatures featured in their cases. One of the shrunken heads, which we familiarly referred to as *la chancha* (the pig), hung from one of the columns in the living room; there were cuckoo clocks about, with the tiny birds that would pop out and state the time, and little doors that would open, from where characters with musical instruments would emerge, just like in Geppetto's house in *Pinocchio*. A crucifix hung on one wall, and a gargoyle's mask faced the stairs on another. The truth is that I never liked to turn around to look at that mask, somehow feeling that its ominous eyes were following me. It is no wonder that my imagination is so wild: Between La Llorona, who would appear in the middle of the night, those tiny heads, and all my father's eccentricities, I developed a vivid imagination; and, of course, not a lot of people get it, but generally speaking, when I allow myself to be led by it, the results are amazing.

There was such an unusual and forceful energy in my house that I believe it was in that place where I began to look inside; I think it happened because I developed a very fast and effective manner of profound introspection, almost as a defense mechanism. I began to communicate with God in that house, so that I would be protected and kept safe in His precious and benevolent company, secure from the presence of anything spooky. I am convinced that our house was built upon very strong energy coordinates, or maybe it is true what people say about the cemetery, because there is no doubt in my mind that the woman dressed in black was the spirit of a dead woman, who was perhaps always crying over her lost children.

And it didn't end there: If you wanted to go for an afternoon nap at around five o'clock in my sisters' room, you would suddenly feel some kind of presence that seemed to lie down on you and render you immobile, and you couldn't scream or ask for help until you prayed that God would save you. According to a Web site that I found while doing a bit of research, modern medicine describes this state as "sleep paralysis, a state of total inability to make any voluntary movements during the initial period of sleep or close to the moment of waking, when one is physically asleep but mentally wide-awake." Some American researchers have concluded that the problem could be a result of certain individuals' susceptibility to electromagnetic phenomenon generated by the earth. So my theory about the house being built on a strongly electromagnetic set of coordinates may not be so far-fetched. . . .

Like any other girl, I invited classmates to come over to my house to play and sleep over, but I would always dread the prospect of one of them seeing or feeling one of these supernatural entities, and in fact, without my telling any of them about it, they would often perceive it on their own. Horrified, they would call their parents, who would have to come and pick them up at two o'clock in the morning . . . my poor friends. Today I'm not sure whether I feel sorry for them or for my mother, who had to get out of bed in her pajamas to hand them—agitated, crying and terrified—back to their parents.

Growing up I never had too many friends, and I think it had a lot to do with the house that we lived in; I was afraid to invite them over, dreading the possibility that something really creepy would happen. When their parents would come to pick them up in the middle of the night, I would be left alone, sad, crying and totally ashamed, mostly because I didn't understand what was going on. Maybe if they had been stronger girls like me, or maybe if they had had a father like mine—with his miniheads in his office and all of his investigations—things might have gone differently.

Because I had very few friends, it made me become closer to my family and the life of my community. It was undoubtedly an amazing group of people, or at least to me it was very special.

Every day I would stroll around the neighborhood with my mother, and my grandmother when she was visiting. We would start by turning the corner of Sabino Street; we would say hello to the newspaperman, who always recognized us, and then we would buy chewing gum, candy, magazines and comic books from him, anything at all. Sometimes we would keep walking until we reached the Dalia market; before we arrived there, we would come upon a series of stands, among them my favorite one, where they sold blue-corn quesadillas about half a meter long. I would order mine filled with white Oaxaca-style cheese, spicy green sauce and . . . total bliss until the very last bite. Later we would systematically cover our route through the market, where my mother would buy everything that she might need for the week: meats, fruits, vegetables, cream, eggs and other products that were sold there. My favorite part was the animal section, where one could buy turtles, little chicks and fish, all of which I in-variably managed to bring home at one point or another. Between the turtle food, the bunnies and the hamsters, my bedroom smelled like a pet store, as I let them all live with me, and they were my sole companions during many days. My mother would burst into my room, furious, and yell, "What a stench! You can't live like this!" Regardless of whether it was cold outside or not, she would immediately open the window to quickly force the smells of chicken, duck, turtle, hamster and fish out of the room. When she noticed that I was cold, she would say, "If you want to have pets, then get used to the cold! You cannot live in such a stinky room!" In the end I chose to stay cold, because all I wanted was to have my little animals with me.

One of the things I loved the most was seeing how the little bunnies, mice and chicks all coexisted along with the butcher, the fruit vendors, the sellers of vegetables and flowers—all of it comprising the family of the market. I always believed that the world was this way: that there were no distinctions or divisions, a world without prejudices. Like many other little kids, I didn't know that there were any countries other than Mexico, or know of any of the differences that society or history had created, like, for example, having a different skin color, speaking a different language, or receiving a different education, all of which I would ultimately learn at school. I suppose the most beautiful thing about being young is . . . being innocent.

Three blocks from my house was the mall of Santa María, and there in its center was the beautiful Moorish kiosk that was designed and built in approximately 1886 to serve as the Mexican pavilion during a world's fair in the city of New Orleans. I would play under its wrought-iron stairs, running through its interiors, staring at its grand columns and walls that could have come out of a Mozarabic poem, like the one by Ruben Dario that my father would recite to us as we lay in his arms, replacing the name of Margarita with one of ours: "*Un kiosco de malaquita, un gran manto de tisú, y una gentil princesita tan bonita, mi Yuyita, tan bonita como tú*" ("A kiosk made of malachite, a great mantle made of tissue, and a gentle princess, so pretty, my Yuyita, so lovely like you"). Yuyita or Yuya was what my father called me after a visit to the Yucatán, because he said there was a bird called the *yuyo* that was known for how beautifully it sings. Who could have known that my nickname was going to serve as such a true premonition?

On weekends, we would regularly visit the parks. I would ride my bicycle around the kiosk, and the atmosphere was always festive—pure Sunday energy: The balloon vendors held tiny plastic whistles in their mouths and would blow them regularly to get the children's attention; the cotton-candy carts with their wooden wheel filled with tons of little holes to place the sticks loaded with cottony treats in blue and pink; and there was a cart that sold ice-cream pops, which would always ring its little bells, that I adored. As soon as we got to the park, I would eat one, and if I was able to convince my mother, I could eat two or three throughout the day.

A Family of Women

Minus the ghosts that haunted my house, I generally had a lovely and active childhood, full of nuances, colors, smells, flavors and music. My family was especially creative, and having four older sisters was like having four private teachers all to myself. We were a gaggle of women, one father, two or three Chihuahuas and all kinds of ghosts.

My oldest sister, Laura, is my mother's daughter from her first marriage, so even though she didn't live with us, we saw her as often as possible. My three other sisters have multiple names, such as Ana Cecilia Luisa Gabriela Fernanda, whom we call Gabi; or Ernestina Leopoldina Amada Ageda Cristina Clementina Patricia, whom we call Titi. With so many older sisters, each of them with their own unique character, and the way they treated me, I always felt like their spoiled little baby.

When the whole family was still together—before my father's

death and before any of my sisters were married—our house was always filled with noise, all sorts of music, makeup everywhere, many styles of clothes, and the rooms were always overflowing with people. My father liked to listen to classical music, such as Bach, Beethoven, Vivaldi, Mozart and Schubert—harmonies that could flush the soul with magnificent sensations. Then suddenly the house would be filled with the sounds of Chabela Vargas, Jorge Negrete, Pedro Vargas and Julio Iglesias; from "Wendolyn" to "Rio Rebelde," we would spend so many afternoons listening to countless songs. And there was no one like my mother, who would combine her favorite artist, the king of rock 'n' roll, Elvis, with Vikki Carr or Gloria Lazo. My grandmother would listen to pieces such as "La Paz, Puerto de Ilusión" and "La Barca de Oro," and one of her favorite versions was by Rafael: "A Mi Manera." And on top of all that, we can't forget my sisters, who practically ran a nightclub out of our house: All day they would play Barry White, Gloria Gaynor, the Rolling Stones, Diana Ross, and Earth, Wind & Fire, along with Sandro de América, Roberto Carlos, Palito Ortega, Camilo Sesto, César Costa, Enrique Guzmán, Alberto Vázquez; my sister Federica loved Violeta Parra, Mercedes Sosa and many other protest singers, which, of course, my father did not like. But for me it was a great discovery when on one of my birthdays, Federica took me to a place called El Mesón de la Guitarra (the Guitar Inn), which was a very famous establishment in the seventies, to see all those musicians with guitars in hand, interpreting songs that depicted a real social context, the young revolutionaries of the time. There, as I sat excitedly in front of those artists who shook us with the rhythm of their music, the innermost desire to do exactly the same took me over and my entire being. From that moment on, I dreamed of facing an audience who would intensely feel what I was singing, of feeling the absolute joy of making them one with the music. What I felt at that moment as a seven-year-old girl was so powerful that to this day it remains etched inside my heart. That was when I realized that this was for me . . . this *is* for me.

To this very day I still love going to the Sanborns restaurant in downtown Mexico City, the one located in the Casa de los Azulejos, where the movement, sound, clinking glasses, screaming and chatting . . . all of it reminds me of the activity that swirled around my house before any of my sisters were married. But it was hard for me to understand how, after I'd had five "mothers"— my four sisters and my mother—as well as my father, my mother and I were suddenly left alone.

Yet that is what happened. As time passed, the house that was once filled with people began to empty out. First, Federica left to get married and live with her husband; later, a year after my father passed away, Ernestina was married in Paris, leaving Gabi and me alone. I played, chatted and ate everything I could dream of with Gabi, as she was always my accomplice, and we had an absolute blast together. However, just one year after Ernestina, Gabi was married as well, when I was almost eight years old. So from that moment on, I was raised alone, as if I were an only child, because the only ones left in the house were my mother, my grandmother and me. Once in a while I would see my nephew, Quetzal, who was kind of like my little brother, and with whom I would take every opportunity to make mischief and satisfy our curiosities. To this day, he still remembers it . . . and boy, does he remember.

For my mother it was hard when my sisters moved away. On top of that, she was left without a man who, like in any other Latin family of the time, had been the financial and emotional backbone of the household. But my mother used the lemons life threw at her to make a delicious lemonade. Once she was able to recover from the loss of my father, she suddenly became a new woman, with a strength that came from the deepest part of her being, giving way to an astonishing sense of inner fortitude that eventually empowered her for the future. After almost two years of mourning, one day she stood up and said to herself, *I am now ready to do what I have always wanted with my life.* And that is exactly what she did.

Until that point, she had been only a mother, who cooked, ironed and essentially ran the home, practically acting as a servant to my father. She was the consummate housewife, but a very incomplete woman nonetheless. My mother was of the classic, old-school type who liked to do menial chores on her own, as she felt these tasks were important to master without reliance or any help from others; she was determined to always feel useful in life. For example, she compulsively polished the black marble living room floor. On her knees, she would lay out the wax on the floor, leaving it to dry so that she could later polish it. Then, when my father got home, he could see his own reflection in the floor like a mirror. She cooked all kinds of different menus: for my sisters, for my father, and on some occasions for herself; and she was only forty years old when she became a widow.

My Mother

My mother was an incredibly strong woman with a powerful character. Like so many women, she learned how to become a manager in her very own home. Having to organize, instruct, distribute, and keep the finances of a household of five daughters—beginning when she was just twenty-five years old—forged a courageous personality; from a superhousewife she ended up becoming the manager of a superstar, and when she started in that role, she had no background whatsoever in the arts world. And if that were not enough, this desire to progress fueled her to become a painter, sculptor and, later, a businesswoman. She was the one who taught me that you can truly have everything you desire, as long as you put in sacrifice, hard work, honesty and loyalty: four values that I still consider to be fundamental to my life today.

From a very young age I was a witness to the exhausting, labor-intensive and sometimes unfulfilling work that comes with running a home. When I saw that it was only at forty years old that my mother actually began to fulfill her own dreams, I decided that I would do everything I could in my own life to never abandon my dreams. So I became determined to succeed as a good human being and professional woman, and waited until I found Mr. Right, a man who would make me feel safe, before having my first child. I always knew that having a child was a huge responsibility, the most beautiful thing that life can give you, and for that reason I wanted to be perfectly sure that I was bringing her into the world at the right moment and with the right person.

There is a lot to learn from the mistakes made by our own mothers; mine even used to say to me, "Honey, there's no rush. It's better to wait to get married; don't make any foolish mistakes, because you have time." When I was married, she would say to me, "Wait a bit before you have a baby; enjoy your marriage and the success of your career." Of course, years later and with more maturity, I understood that it wasn't such a good idea to wait so long, nor to do exactly what other people tell you to do. If I had been able to see the future through a crystal ball, and had found out how difficult it would be to have my first child, I might have done a few things differently.

Life throws us unexpected twists that we are genuinely not ready to face, whether the death of a loved one, illness or, in my case, unexpected fame. Now I understand how enriched I am because of some of the most challenging moments that I had to endure as a little girl; all those experiences made me who I am today. Losing my hero, my father; becoming famous when I was just a teen and living in the public eye; the pressure on a young girl to always be "perfect"; this is what my days were like: full of expectations, demands, the pursuit of perfection and ambition.

All of this taught me a lot. The most useful lesson I learned was that sometimes I had to say no whenever things didn't sit well with me, especially if I was doing them for the sake of pleasing someone else. I learned to listen to myself, to listen to the little voice inside myself that said, *Whom do you want to impress today? What else do you want out of life? Why do you need more? Whom are you doing this for? For them? Or for you?*

All of us go through moments of uncertainty and confusion when people talk to us and when they don't, when they have opinions and when they have nothing to say, so it is normal that even our consciousness will get distracted from time to time. We are, after all, humans. Not robots. But ultimately it is wonderful to find balance in your life; it might be difficult, yes, but certainly not impossible.

I was always a very creative child; I used to make up my own games, and even my own toys and my own stories. I would spend hours alone while my mother was at the Academy of San Carlos, the art school where she took lessons. When I returned home from school, alone in the house I would give free rein to my imagination and in that way became a creative, imaginative and dreamy type of girl. It was hard for me to separate fantasy from reality, perhaps because it was better to dream than to actually feel the reality of my solitude.

I had to face another situation when I learned the second

great lesson of my life, one that I had to comprehend the hard way: dead-on, without any time to think about it. It marked me profoundly. I was around seven years old when a cousin of mine asked if I would go outside with her, where all the neighborhood kids were playing. There were some kids our age having fun on a merry-go-round, but one of the older ones would not let me join in and said, "Not her—her father just died. . . . She can't play with us!" All the other kids started laughing at me while chanting, "The girl who doesn't have a father! The girl who doesn't have a father!" I didn't understand what was happening or what I was feeling, but I could not stop thinking, *How can they be so mean?* It was the first time that I felt such a punch to the gut; it was as if my heart were weeping inside, a deep pain that grew at the base of my belly. It was my first face-to-face encounter with evil, with malicious and toxic people, and it came from a group of children. Of course, children are not aware of the damage that they can do to other kids, but for me that moment was pure agony.

It is not easy to be mature at an early age. In my case, not having a kid brother or sister with whom to share, play and fight made me into a very lonely little girl. Also, it felt as if everything around me was always changing. My mother began to flourish after the death of my father, the moment she released the shackles that kept her trapped inside a simple life, which had absolutely nothing to do with her actual dreams. I think that if she were given the chance to do it all over again, my mother wouldn't have gotten married until the age of forty. Maybe she wouldn't have had any children. She was not a conventional woman, but she lived encaged in my grandmother's beliefs of what a woman *should* be, and what Mexican society expected at the time. The truth is that my mother was no princess. It's more like she turned into Cinderella without even realizing what was going on around her. But

I am convinced that this submissive attitude pushed her to be the fierce woman that she was until the day she passed. Because nobody could stop my mother. Especially no man!

And regardless of how brilliant and successful he was, my father was no knight in shining armor. He was not an easy man, very macho, and he held my mother back most of the time, perhaps because she was a wildly beautiful woman. She was so stunning that anyone who laid eyes on her would think she belonged to the golden era of movie stars. Her beauty was striking, and my father would die of jealousy just thinking about the prospect of someone coming on to her. And this is how her life, her world, ultimately turned into a routine: from the house to the market, from the house to the girls' school, from the house to the church, and occasionally to the movies with the girls, and right back to the house. My father would even time how long it took her to get from one place to the next, which I now realize was insane! That's why, when he passed away, my mother—while of course very sad—also felt a great amount of relief and liberation. She realized that there was something amazing out there that she had never really had the chance to know. Something she had never had access to, God knows why.

From being a totally submissive woman, my mother transformed into a woman who dealt as an equal with the highest-ranking television executives, for example. Overnight she became my manager, and her attitude became, *Get out of my way, because now you're going to see who Yolanda Miranda is. No one will ever humiliate me again.* She was indestructible.

Discovering the Artist Within

I am convinced that these life circumstances led me to become an artist, but as much as I adore my profession, sometimes I feel a little like a fish out of water. I have always felt a bit uncomfortable in show business, especially because I am not the kind of person who likes to show off. I also don't like to talk about myself. My mother often told me that I had to learn how to "throw it around" and not seem so incredulous about my own success. But it was the hand of destiny itself that brought me to where I am now in life. Whether or not I am able to believe in my successes, there are still a lot of things about this profession that I hate, such as having to be far from my loved ones, always working, always promoting, always smiling, even when on the inside I am really exhausted.

But at the end of the day, what I love to do is sing, write songs, spend hours in the studio with my fellow musicians creating sounds and new musical possibilities, making momentary magic, cadenced and harmonic tones and sounds that will exist forever. It thrills me to think that these songs could serve to keep a person company during some of the most important moments of their lives: at their wedding, at their *quinceañera,* during their moments of shame, success or love. It is exciting for me to be on a stage and to feel the audience so alive, smell them, touch them, singing the songs that were one day just a simple idea and a chorus, now sung out loud vigorously with thousands of voices singing along at a show. What I love is to live among my diverse fans in different parts of the world, getting to know one another personally, and really talking to everyone—not to mention how amazing it feels to play a character that actually shakes me to the core.

To me, this is the magic of my profession. . . . This is life. . . . This is me screaming through every pore of my being, *I am alive . . . I am here . . . I am complete . . . I am me.*

I love art—its creation and expression. When that magical part of my career gets fogged over by rumors or the distorted images that often get concocted about artists, it's hard for me to understand what it is that really bothers people; the whole thing gets stuck in my throat, because I just don't know how to digest it; it simply doesn't flow. That's the part of my work that's far from what I've always dreamed about. Nevertheless, I managed to prevail by swimming against the current, clearing off the algae, the branches and the traps that have been set to "eliminate" me. But you know what? No one can eliminate a light, even though its luminescence might bother some. It's just like one of my fans said to me one day: "My queen, if your light bothers them, let them wear sunglasses!"

Since social networks have taken over the world, I feel a lot more at peace with my relationship with the media. I thank God that I can communicate with my fans directly, and see their reactions in real time; I can talk to them about everything, and wish them a good night, and even tell them what Lyme disease is all about. I find social networks to be beneficial because they turn every person into his or her very own reporter, which is very liberating.

I should clarify that no social networks, nor the many experts of whom I sought help in search of answers, are necessarily responsible for my peace of mind. The key is to accept yourself exactly as you are, because we spend our whole lives wanting to change or become someone who we believe is somehow more perfect than ourselves, without being clear about our true potential, who we are, how we can modify and improve certain attitudes and thoughts to extract the best of ourselves and truly shine. The moment that I realized this, everything changed for the better. I stopped seeing everything from the outside, superficially, and I began to really look at myself from within, to know and accept my limitations, and to understand that there will be certain times when I will be at the top, and other times when it will be someone else's turn. This allows me to understand how important it is to feel the freedom to say no.

I was such a people pleaser that in the course of my career, whenever I was presented with a new project, without thinking about it, without reviewing it, I would immediately say yes just to please the producer, the businessman or the manager (who was my mother, of course!).

In the documentary that we filmed for *Primera Fila* (*First Row*), my latest album, which came out in 2009, there is a moment when the interviewer takes me on a tangent: from the most intimate place of my being, I confessed to him that all I want to do is sing like I did when I was a little girl; I needed to look that girl in the eyes and reconnect with her. That is how the idea of this book came to be, as a way of moving from the past to the present, and saving that girl-woman so that she can have a solid future.

Thalia, the little girl, has to come back to me.

The time has finally come to reconnect with the silent girl from my past who thought that her father had died because of her last kiss to him—because everything has changed. I embraced her; I rescued her; I forgave her; with every part of my being I told her, "I love you. . . . You won't miss out on anything. . . . Don't worry about the future. . . . I am here. . . . Everything is going to be okay."

I embraced myself. . . . I rescued myself. . . . I forgave myself.

Because a major part of accepting yourself is forgiving and I was very hard on myself, an unwavering judge of my own actions. We are our worst judges, and we give ourselves the worst punishments. And if you are a Virgo, it's even worse!

Throughout this whole process I have also learned . . .

To let go of what I cannot change.

To accept what I cannot change.

To stop trying to control what is uncontrollable.

How to say, "Llorona . . . I no longer fear you."

CHAPTER TWO

FAME

D

ear Fame:

A four-letter word that moves millions of souls, that charts a "perfect" path, inviting magnificent smiles from those who, in some way, manage to cross paths with you.

Who isn't seduced by your ever-delicate and exquisite charms, which are all displayed in a flash of lights, riches, success and total glory?

You enthrall your students with such subtlety that they see only what you want them to see, hear what you want them to hear, and in return you offer up the total crystallization of their dreams.

What a perfect deception: You steal your students from the world in which they were born, and you take them to live in a world fabricated by applause, praise and power, allowing them to feel the sense of strength and security in knowing that every desire is taken into consideration, exactly as you projected.

But you also know how to run away as soon as the project doesn't come through, when dreams and desires are shattered; you, Fame, vanish; you leave for a while, leaving your "victim" in the grasp of total solitude, confusion, helplessness and discouragement—giving way to another uninvited guest: depression.

But since everything that goes up must come down, and everything that goes down inevitably also comes up, the time to be up returns again, and you show up like an overenthusiastic old friend who hasn't been around for a while.

You hug, you kiss, you flatter, you entertain, you exalt and you caress as if nothing at all had happened, and only those who mature through the catastrophe, the pain, the mockery and the unrest caused by your indifference emerge secure in this new phase of life, in which you continue to be around.

Fame, you will always be connected to my name. One day you invited me to walk by your side; now I invite you—but this time on my own terms.

It is impossible to separate us, so walk along with me and discover my nuances, many various facets and the ample perspective that has come with maturity.

Fame, you stand in the face of a very complete and secure human being. . . . Take my hand, and get to know who I really am.

The Birth of Power, Glory and Fame

I entered show business very early in life: My first encounter
with television cameras was at the age of three. My father used to
appear on a program called *Estudiantinas Que Estudian* (*Student
Clubs That Study*), asking questions of the different student
groups competing for first place. One day, as the show was being
taped live, he brought me in dressed up in the cape of an *estudi-
antina,* and I appeared on air with the conductor, Gustavo Ferrer,
in front of dozens of children who played instruments and sang
along with great enthusiasm.

But it was at the age of five that I began to work professionally:
I made my first appearance as an extra in a film called *La Guerra
de los Pasteles* (*War of Cakes*), a musical comedy directed by René
Cardona and produced by Angélica Ortiz, which depicted the his-
toric battles between the armies of Mexico and France in 1838.
My sister Laura was acting in the movie, and she would invite me

to come see all the different sets that had been built. I was noticed because I was able to act naturally, as if the scenes I was in were a part of everyday life. I wore a period costume from the late nineteenth century, replete with crinoline and gigantic ruffles, gloves with a trim of pearl buttons, and big satin bows in my hair. I was positioned behind some of the main actors in a few scenes. I will never forget when my mother showed me a little piece of paper that said *Cincuenta pesos*, and hearing her say, "My little girl, your first paycheck, which you earned for your work . . . Congratulations, my love! Now what do you want to do with it?" Of course, my answer was, "La Cubana, Mami, La Cubana . . . Take me to La Cubana." La Cubana, my favorite chocolatier, had been in my neighborhood since the turn of the century. There were massive glass jars filled with little pills, which were really tiny little bags of colored sugar in whimsical shapes. The whole place had a sweet, chocolaty smell that I will always have etched into my memory. So with that first paycheck I bought little bunnies, cars, cigarettes, cigars, rings and pencils—everything made of chocolate. It was a veritable feast.

When I was about seven years old, I joined the cast of a morning variety program called *La Mujer Ahora* (*Women Now*) on Televisa, one of the largest Mexican networks, where children played a major role. The hostess, Evelyn Lapuente, was a young, jovial blonde with fantastic bangs; she was the Mexican Jane Fonda, and if I remember correctly, the director of children's programming was Sergio Andrade, who years later was linked to one of the biggest scandals in the Mexican entertainment industry. I loved participating in all the different parts of the program, which were created by children for children at home: We sang; we would model; we wore costumes. On one occasion they even dressed me up as a geisha. It was strange for me to catch a glimpse of myself in the studio monitors, to see the image that was broadcast on televisions across the country. Every time I looked at the monitors I felt butterflies in my belly, and I would get the urge to giggle nervously—those were my first emotions when it came to appearing on television.

My favorite part of the show was the section about cooking. It was when they would allow us to prepare food, for which my mother, who was a great chef, taught me how to make quick and delicious meals for the show. It's a shame I didn't have time afterward to learn how to elaborate on those different dishes from Mexican, Japanese and Italian kitchens. My mother spoiled me so much that she would never let me do anything myself, and she would do everything for me in the kitchen. "That's why you have a mother," she would always say to me. The fact that I didn't know how to cook never stopped me from enjoying food, no matter where it came from. I like everything; I eat everything; I enjoy everything, and I am thankful to God because today I have the opportunity to enjoy, savor and delight in those moments when I can sit at a table and dig into a good plate of food surrounded by pleasant company. No one can take the epicurean out of me; I can guarantee you that eating is my number one hobby.

My first encounter with fame happened at home, in 1977, a year that profoundly impacted my family and brought a lot of joy and some very deep sorrow, as well. Laura won first prize in the children's theatrical adaptation of the play *Ifigenia en Tauride*, which played at the Cervantino Festival in Guanajuato, the city of mummies. Then Ernestina was nominated as Miss Federal District, and served as the alternate to Miss Mexico, and also earned the title of Miss Continental; she competed in Japan, and won as Miss Kimono one day after my birthday. Federica was married in August, and a few months later, in November, my father passed away. It was a very intense year, a year that affected our lives forever.

I will never forget the night that Titi won the title of Miss Federal District. Since I was a little girl, my parents didn't want me to attend such a crowded event that went on so late, so that night all the women in my house—the beauty queen, my mother and my sisters—went to the event while my father and I stayed at home, anxiously awaiting their arrival. When Ernestina walked in she looked so joyful that I saw the sunshine slip in behind her; she was radiant, her entire being emanating a certain brilliance—she looked stunning. My father wore the crown and the cape and toted the scepter throughout the house, proud of his little girl's triumph. But in the midst of the celebration and the carrying-on, he noticed me sitting at the marble table observing him. He walked over to where I was sitting, removed the cape that was the same turquoise blue as my sister's eyes, and placed it over my little shoulders. I felt so important! And when he placed the crown on my head and the scepter in my hands, in that exact moment I was jolted with the urge to win—to win what, I didn't know— but to win so that I could be as important as my sister was that night. I saw how all eyes were always on her, how all the congratulations were for her, and how her happiness was reflective of others' happiness. . . . At that moment, I wanted to be exactly like my sister; I wanted to be famous. Fame walked in attached to the crook of Titi's arm, complete with crown, cape and scepter, and waltzed into my family's life, becoming a central part of it, and later becoming my own clingy best friend, at once demanding and implacable.

Music

Music has always been a great part of my life, and since I was raised around so many of its genres and forms, I developed an educated selectivity for it, allowing me to evolve my own personal melodic predilections from an early age. When I was about seven, there was a musical group that I liked a lot, comprised of Spanish children, called Parchis. I knew all of their songs, and, watching them on television, I was able to learn all their dance routines. That was when Laura told my mother that one of her friends, Paco Ayala, was putting together a children's group, and that auditions were being held at a club called Peerless, which was famous then for exclusively featuring the incomparable singer Pedro Infante, who to this day remains my idol. We drove to the auditions right away, and when they told me what I had to sing, I gave it my all. Then they told me to wait in a room, and minutes later I was a member of the group, along with two boys and a girl—Paquito, Alejandro and Valeria. The original name of the group was PacMan, and our theme song alluded to the group's name, which was a famous video game character at the time. Pac-Man was the most popular game for an entire generation of people all over the world. With our name we were able to ride the wave of Pac-Man's popularity so that everyone sang along with us: "*Es pequeño y redondito con la boca grande y quiere comer, y le gustan las golosinas, y también los malvaviscos, tiene tanta hambre que todo se engullirá . . . ese es Pac-Man*" ("That little round guy with the big mouth wants to eat; he loves candy and marshmallows; he's so hungry he engulfs everything . . . that's Pac-Man").

But just a short time after we began, some copyright issues came up, so we had to change our name, and we ultimately became Grupo Din Din. We recorded an ample repertoire that later turned into four albums. We would rehearse all our dances in my garage with my yellow Hello Kitty boom box, which was my contribution; our nascent collective had a very tight budget! Even so, we were able to travel from village to village, touring with our children's act everywhere around Mexico. We did this during our vacations and holidays, on weekends and in summer, so that we wouldn't miss school. Back then I studied at the Franco-Mexican Lyceum, and that was always my priority—to continue with my studies. This particular schedule was not difficult to accommodate with our manager, since our education was also very much a priority for him. That's why rehearsals were always held after classes and once we had finished our homework.

On one Easter holiday, the idea came up for us to perform in one of the most famous beach resorts in Mexico. "We're going to Acapulco," the producers told us one day. "We will be performing at the Marriott hotel. . . . Kids, you're going to do great." Until then, our shows had typically been small and modest, so this would mean a whole new investment in wardrobe, and the development of a new act. It was a tremendous opportunity for our group, because an important and reputable hotel chain was hiring us. So we went to Acapulco very enthusiastically, because in addition to plans for performing our new act, thoughts of beach vacations swirled around in our minds, and we dreamed of soaking and splashing around in the ocean. But the time we spent in Acapulco ended up being quite the opposite. Vacation? Maybe for everyone else. For us, it was time to work.

Since it was Easter, Acapulco was bursting. Part of our job was to promote the show, so every day from eleven in the morning until one in the afternoon, we were dressed up like little clowns, with wigs, red noses, brightly colored shoes and the classic long-sleeved pin-striped overalls with cotton pom-poms that stuck out like buttons on our chests. They had us walk the whole beach in these outfits, and the sand would creep into our shoes, the merciless rays of the sun would burn us through our wigs, and our makeup would melt off and drip into our eyes. It didn't matter what condition we were in; we had to distribute flyers so that people would come see us perform—while we watched the rest of the kids having fun on the beach, getting in the water and enjoying their vacations. But recreation was not an option for us. Right after dinner, we were already up onstage, singing and dancing our best repertoire for the kids gathered in the room, while their parents went off shopping, or out for a piña colada or some other refreshing libation. This little show was like a breath of fresh air for the parents, when they could fully relax while we entertained their children.

Our great opportunity came up when Televisa launched a new kids' show that made it into millions of homes, creating a huge sensation among the children and adolescents everywhere in the country. The show was called *Juguemos a Cantar* (*Let's Play Singing*), a children's equivalent of what we know today as *American Idol* or *The X Factor*. From a pool of thousands, we made it on as contestants, and I found myself for the first time as a singer on a television screen, watching the movements of the cameras and people moving around behind the scenes. The audience eagerly awaited the onset of the show, which was, of course, live, while the four of us, with our parents' help, tried to calm the butterflies that frantically flew around in our stomachs.

The emcee, with his loud and powerful voice, announced, "And now, with you . . . Diiiiinnn Diiiinnnn!" The room filled with applause and we began singing "*Somos Alguien Muy Especial*" ("We Are Very Special"). I was consumed with nerves, and my legs felt like they were made of jelly. I focused on the faces of the people in the studio audience, who watched with great attention and clapped along, which helped to gradually dissolve my anxiety as we made our way through the song.

We ended up doing very well, which led to myriad new work opportunities. From that moment on, we performed in various places all over the country, mostly on Saturdays and Sundays, for family entertainment. Our weekend tours went on for about a year, and shortly thereafter the group broke up, since each one of us went off to a different school and it became harder for us to find a time to practice.

Regardless, my mother did not allow my career to stop there. She hustled with such gusto that one day she came home and, without great preamble, announced, "Honey, get ready, because you are going to compete as a soloist in *Juguemos a Cantar,* and we already have a song for you—it's called 'Modern Rock Girl.' So it is time to get to work on arrangements and choreography!" And with that I began to practice. My mother had two great floor-to-ceiling mirrors installed on the doors of my closets. In front of them, with my beloved Hello Kitty boom box nearby, I began to develop my own choreography, using the demo given to me by the record label that sold the official sound track to the show. I also worked on creating the costume that I envisioned myself wearing. I pictured great pointed shoulder pads, something really futuristic, outer space–like, made of a purple liquidlike Lycra fabric. I, of course, wanted to pay homage to one of my favorite artists of the time, Prince, and his *Purple Rain.* Between sheets of blank paper, my sketches, my colored pencils everywhere and my songs playing at full volume, my dream was turning into reality. The day of the competition—dressed in purple in a design of my own, with purple sequined leggings, and with the dance troupe that the producer had selected to accompany me in the choreography that I had developed in the magical world of my bedroom—I came out with a mission to captivate that audience, who responded with great applause. When the show was over, I was among the top five contestants, and the next day all the newspapers wrote about the "Rock Girl" who had won the hearts of the audience with her act. On the way home, I could feel the same joy and magic that Titi felt when she was crowned as beauty queen. But in this case, my crown and my scepter were the applause and the love that came from the audience.

In the summer of that year, the musical *Vaselina*—based on the movie *Grease,* starring John Travolta and Olivia Newton-John—was playing in Mexico City. Julissa, a Mexican actress of great renown, had done the adaptation. All the actors in the lead roles were from a famous Mexican kids' band called Timbiriche. (They were like today's cast of *Glee,* or the most famous stars who started out on a Disney Channel series.) All the kids my age were fans of Timbiriche, so on my birthday I asked my mother to take me to the theater to see *Vaselina.*

A few days earlier, my mom was in the office of the ANDY and the ANDA, which are organizations that protect the rights of actors and singers in Mexico, and ran into Julissa, and she jumped on the opportunity to tell her about my birthday, and that my present would be to go and see the play. My mother asked her to please save two good seats for us. Julissa did just as my mom asked, and left precise instructions to reserve us two of the best seats, close to the stage and in the middle of the auditorium.

As I focused on Sandy's transformation from wholesome good girl to sassy rebel, my mom leaned over to me and said into my ear, "One day you will be the one wearing that leather jacket. . . . You'll see." All I could reply was, "Shhhhhh, Mama. You're not letting me listen."

When the show was over, I went backstage to say hello to one of my friends, who was a singer in the chorus, which was when I ran into Julissa, along with her scenic director, Marta Zabaleta.

"Hey, aren't you the one who sang 'Modern Rock Girl'?" asked Marta.

When I told her I was, she didn't hesitate with her proposition: "I have some auditions coming up. Why don't you come by to try out?"

And that was just how it was. That week I went in for an audition. With all my mother's hopes and my own anxiety, I got up onstage, sang and delivered the monologue that they gave me for the tryout. I felt satisfied with what I did; for some reason I was no longer nervous, and somewhere deep inside I knew that I had made it in. I passed the audition and they first placed me in the chorus, where I was what we playfully referred to as "tree number three" or "shadow B"—in other words the filler, the last one in the choir. Later on I would take on some of the secondary roles. But just from watching the show so much, I learned all the actors' lines and the whole show from start to finish. All the blocking, every gesture, the dances, the pauses . . . everything.

I continued with my work playing some of the secondary characters that were assigned to me, until one day someone said to me, "Marta Zabaleta is looking for you."

I got excited, because I knew that Sasha, the girl who played the role of Sandy, had to deal with some personal matters that were going to make her absent from the show for a few days.

As I sat in her office, she looked at me directly in the eyes and said, "Would you like to play the role of Sandy?"

"Me?" I answered, completely flustered. Could what I was

hearing be possible? Was the director telling me that I could play the lead role? My head was spinning with excitement. "Of course!" I added, trying to contain my emotion. "When?"

Without a missing a beat, the director said, "Tomorrow . . . Do you really think you can do it?"

And without even stopping to think about it, I said, "Yes!"

That very night, and for the first time in my life, I suffered a massive migraine that left me in the hospital for several hours. I had to urgently be sedated intravenously to help me sleep, so that I could endure the worst part of the migraine episode.

But the very next day, I kept my word and showed up for work. I was Sandy.

When I donned that black leather jacket as Sandy transformed from sweetheart to panther, I remembered that moment when I was sitting in the audience with my mother and she whispered to me, "One day you will be the one wearing that leather jacket. . . ." Prophecy was indeed fulfilled.

From that moment on, I played the role of Sandy whenever Sasha could not be there. Later on, during the play's second run without Timbiriche, I kept the role, and starred alongside Benny Ibarra, in the role of Danny.

After six hundred performances and the show's great success, the renowned producer Luis de Llano spoke with my mother about the possibility of my joining Timbiriche. Sasha was leaving the group for personal reasons and they needed a replacement. De Llano liked my interpretation of Sandy in the show and wanted to offer me the job. And there began a new chapter of my artistic career, and a whole new series of challenges that I never could have imagined. The first one was that I joined the band as some kind of intruder among a clique of kids who had already formed a small family of their own. I paid a high price for being the new girl, and to be allowed to become a member of the group.

At that time, Timbiriche was at the pinnacle of its popularity and I would have been crazy to turn down the chance to join. But the contract Luis de Llano presented to my mother basically said that she was renouncing her rights as my manager for television, images, video, voice, merchandising—anything that had to do with the Timbiriche brand—and that I would have to travel alone with the band like the other kids, under the care of the group's manager. Well, my mother did not like that condition one bit, so a family meeting was held to discuss the matter. My mother said that if she was not permitted to stick by my side she would not allow me to be a part of the group; Titi said that I should be sent to a Swiss boarding school; and Laura said it was an amazing opportunity. Everyone had an opinion, and the family was divided. All I did was cry as I watched my dreams seemingly disintegrate just as I was finally reaching them. My tears and pleading did nothing to make my mother budge—if she was not allowed to accompany me everywhere, she was simply not going to allow me to participate. That's exactly what she said to Luis de Llano, and he, without flinching, accepted. He agreed to her accompanying me on all my trips, but he warned her about the accommodations, the inflexible schedules and the lack of luxuries. My mother did not care about any of those things; she just wanted to ensure that her young daughter wasn't traveling around the world all alone—and she accepted.

And so began the great Timbiriche adventure.

Being Timbiriche, we lived in a world that was totally surreal. We were given everything we asked for, we could get anything at all, and we were untouchable, powerful, almost like little gods.

Everyone wanted to be around Timbiriche, to touch Timbiriche, to be a part of Timbiriche. . . .

Initially, Timbiriche was formed as a counter to popular groups like Parchis, or Menudo from Puerto Rico, but with more of a pop sound, and six charismatic kids dressed up in colorful outer-space costumes. Initially the group was called the Timbiriche Band, comprised of Benny Ibarra, Sasha Sokol, Diego Schoening, Paulina Rubio, Mariana Garza and Alix Bauer; the whole concept was attractive to a children's market that was hungry for something new. With the album covers, the band logo and the songs themselves, the band unleashed a passion in millions and millions of kids. Later on, new members to the group came on board, such as Erik Rubin. When Benny and Sasha left the band, Eduardo Capetillo and I joined the group, and that was when the group's name became simply Timbiriche. Costumes were a bit more daring back then, lyrics were more powerful, and from children we went on to become teenagers, with all the force of our youth, growing right alongside our fans.

My mom was the only mother who traveled with the band. We spent entire days on vans, nibbling snacks along the way, and sleeping while we were on the road. My mother endured it all, and I believe that the fact of her being near me during those first few years saved me from being devoured by the wolves that circled us looking for young talent to prey on. Even so, for the rest of the band the whole thing was quite odd and incomprehensible: "Why is this woman here with that new girl who replaced Sasha? Why is she watching everything we do? What is this intruder doing here?" The other members of the group raised their voices in protest, which caused a lot of bickering among us, and problems during my first weeks with the group. I got my fair share of dirty looks, nasty attitudes, glares, backstabbing, mockery and, more than anything, the total indifference of the girls. Because I was the new girl, the guys would argue about who would win me over. That was the part that made things tricky; it was amusing to have Diego ask me out for a burger, and then arrive home to find flowers sent by Capetillo, while Erik sat next to me during the dance rehearsals and spoke to me with great zeal, his eyes alive and flirtatious. My entry into the group was hard, but I was able to understand the love and the bond they shared, and later, with the wisdom of time, I got to feel it myself and experience such lovely camaraderie.

But in the beginning the girls really made me suffer. Mariana was the most mature for her age, always looking at things objectively and from a balanced perspective. She was my roommate and was always very sweet with me, and during the time that I was in the group, she was a great source of support for me. Alix lived in her own world, so much that she barely noticed my presence; and I think that it was most difficult for Paulina to accept me, since she had lost Sasha, who was her best friend. Sasha and Paulina were the same astrological sign, they shared the same birthday, and they were very close friends, almost like sisters, so naturally Sasha's surprise departure from the group didn't sit well with Paulina at all, and much less so when another girl was coming in to "replace" her best friend. That was why it was so hard for us in the beginning, but later we went on to have a warm friendship filled with lots of love.

As months passed, I started to become like a fish in water as far as the group went, and my mom started to feel more comfortable with our tour management. So she gradually let me travel on my own on trips that primarily took place in Mexico and later went on to other parts of Central and South America. At the end of 1987 and early 1988, the group began to go on larger-scale tours, with the surge of success that came with the devotion of our teenage fans. Entire months would pass before we came home to change our clothes. Everywhere we went we were followed by legions of fans (some even followed us from city to city), and entire floors in hotels were reserved for us. We became famous before we truly understood what fame was, and all of that awoke a false sense of empowerment. We began to see the power we held, and, of course, our first instinct was to abuse it. I remember, for example, one occasion when the whole band had some time off, and we were lying around the hotel room watching movies. Since we couldn't go out, and we really had nothing to do but sit in front of the television, somebody said, "I'm hungry. . . . Let's order some food." Another one said, "What should we order?" To which a third one responded, "The whole menu!" So with no worry in the world, we picked up the phone and ordered everything from room service. Everything. Moments later, aluminum trays with covers began to appear, containing salads, soups, meats, chicken, hamburgers, desserts, ice creams . . . and for what? Just so that we could nibble and sample from everything. It was total culinary excess.

We were a group of kids on the brink of entering puberty, our hormones were raging, and the energy that emanated from our pores was an infinite source of ideas that needed to, somehow or another, be expressed. Our lives were not normal, and with the exception of when we were doing shows or rehearsing, we were almost always locked up in a room, like lions in captivity—so we channeled our intensity in all kinds of ways. Sometimes we would set off the fire extinguishers in the hotels and run loose in the hallways in our pajamas at two a.m. One time, just to quell the extreme boredom that consumed us, we decided to throw the musicians' luggage over the balcony and into the hotel pool. As the cases plummeted, clothes went flying everywhere, draping and falling all over the tree branches and inside the pool. That's how we experienced a form of escape, through childhood mischief. Since we spent most of our time in hotels and working, we had to do something in order not to lose our minds and to reclaim our youth, and it was just these types of escapades that allowed us to keep being what we were: kids, preadolescent kids with power . . . with a lot of power.

By then I had already dropped out of school, the Franco-Mexican Lyceum, having just completed middle school, and Timbiriche's managers were able to find a more flexible school for us so that we could continue with our education in Mexico City. So when we weren't traveling, we went on with our studies.

Television

During one of those weeks when we had time off while we were in Mexico, my mother and I received an unexpected call: Carla Estrada, a producer of one of the most popular soap operas of the time, had a proposition. I remember it perfectly, because I watched as my mother, glued to the phone, paid rapt attention to everything the producer said.

"I want your daughter in my soap opera," she said. "I'd like to set her up with casting; please stop by."

So we went. The producers met us in the foyer where the filming was taking place for *La Pobre Señorita Limantour* (*Poor Miss Limantour*), the show in which the producer wanted me to take a role. When she saw us, she immediately started talking to me about the project, what it was about and what awaited me. . . . That was when I realized that Carla had no intention of putting me through an audition. She had already decided—she wanted me for her show. I became nervous, seeing how sure of herself she was as she spoke to me, so at the first opportunity I said, "Carla, I'm a theater actress. The truth is that I have never seen the inner workings of a television studio, and I have no idea what's happening behind or in front of the cameras."

She smiled and with a confident gesture said, "Don't worry; I'll teach you. If you like, let's start the training tomorrow. Come to the stage in the morning and you'll see that it's not hard at all. If you have done theater, and you have had to convince the very last person in the final row, television is more compact. It's magical; with just one look you are capable of anything and everything. Do you know what a prompter is?"

"No, I have absolutely no idea what a prompter is," I answered.

So Carla smiled again and confirmed our appointment for the next day. I sat in a chair behind the cameras, and with the prompter at my ear, I watched as each scene of the soap opera unfolded, one after another. That's how I learned what a prompter is—a small device that is placed in your ear, and through which your lines are delivered, as well as your blocking and motions. I was impressed to see how the actors took direction and said their lines, giving it all their own style. It was amazing to see how they transformed the instructions they were given to create living characters made of flesh and bone. Carla was right: Television was magical.

"I want to give you an exercise that you should do regularly," Carla said. "Listen to the radio, and repeat everything you hear on the station that you choose—just keep repeating everything; this will teach you how to work with a prompter."

And from that moment on, on the way to rehearsals or interviews or to my house, regardless of where I was, I was plugged into my earphones and, like a parrot, repeated everything that I heard.

Since I was a little girl I had always been determined to keep my word, which was why I expressed my concerns before committing to the soap opera on top of the commitment I already had to the group. The thing that worried me the most was being able to measure up as a television actress while keeping up my role in the group. Once again, Carla was able to appease me: "Don't worry, Thalia. Yours is a small role, so you will have to shoot only two days a week."

Even so, the character continued to develop, because people liked her so much; and as the character kept evolving, so, too, did my obligation with the soap opera. Two days a week turned into three and four, until *La Pobre Señorita Limantour* ended in 1987. That was my debut in the world of soaps. Carla Estrada was a great teacher, and with her help I came face-to-face with television studios. I learned how to use a prompter, among so many other important and valuable lessons as I entered the world of television and acting.

Nonetheless, as my acting career continued to flourish, I continued to work full steam ahead with Timbiriche. It was like working two jobs, because sometimes I would leave the studio and, without even a moment of rest but only grabbing a quick bite on the way, I would be taken directly to some performance where all the members of Timbiriche were slated to appear. Many times the band would already have one foot on the stage when I showed up abruptly to change my clothes and join the group during the first few chords of the song. Those were, without a doubt, very intense years of training, and this was precisely when I developed my rigid—but multifaceted—professional structure that has, to this day, made me adaptable to each and every kind of work I do. It was when I learned how to become a chameleon who, despite the pressure, always follows through on a commitment.

The next year, filming began for the telenovela *Quinceañera,* and once again Carla Estrada put her faith in me and gave me a role in this wonderful project on which the TV company was betting big. This was a more serious commitment, because it was a lead role alongside the actress Adela Noriega, darling of the soap opera world and young people in general at that time. The commitment entailed working Monday through Friday, with many scenes per day, so it became a lot harder for me to continue my work with Timbiriche. The soap took up all my time, giving me only windows in which I could join the group when they were performing on Fridays through Sundays. Since the Timbiriche shows and *Quinceañera* both aired on Televisa, it was a lot easier to coordinate schedules and plan trips, shows and recordings. I felt the support of my peers in the group; I never got so much as a dirty look or any sense of resentment from them regarding my decision to simultaneously work as a television actress.

The first day of filming, I was put in a dressing room with three actresses whose work was quite different from mine—they would spend only a few hours in the studio, while I, as a lead character, practically spent the whole day at Televisa. In light of the situation, my mother asked whether I could have my own dressing room so that I could rest between scenes.

"No, Yolandita," they said a few times, "there are no available dressing rooms. That's how it is—everything is full and there is no way to move Thalia into another dressing room."

"No problem," my mom said, and for three weeks she had me change in the main bathroom of the studio. She told them, "If she doesn't have a dressing room, then what else are we going to do . . . and if she has to change in the main bathroom until the end of the show, well, so be it. . . . And if she has to wait for her cue on the extras' bench and in the dressing rooms located at the foot of the studio, that's how she will do it." The point that my mom was making with her request was that if there were two *quinceañeras* and two protagonists, how could one of them have a dressing room to herself while the other had to share hers with three other actresses? What my mother sought was equality. It wasn't just the fact that we had the same size role; what my mother wanted was for me to have a space to come back to—it didn't matter how big it was—and rest between scenes. A space that would be my own and that I wouldn't have to share with three other actresses who were clearly not on the same exhausting schedule I was.

Pretty soon I got my own dressing room, which felt like heaven, given how badly I needed to rest from the stress of the dual workload of the soap opera and Timbiriche.

My face appeared every afternoon in millions of Mexican households. Timbiriche performed the show's theme song, also called "*Quinceañera.*" This was a strategy devised by the executives to combine the momentum of Timbiriche with the first soap opera directed toward a younger audience, and for which Televisa had high hopes.

When the filming for the soap was completed, I thanked Timbiriche and parted ways with them, as I was starting to have an even busier work schedule, and I didn't want to let anyone down. Also, I had to face my desire to become a solo act.

Every time I was onstage with the group, my imagination would go wild and I would imagine that everyone was there to see my show, to watch me perform as a soloist. Everyone around me seemed to disappear, and I would imagine myself alone with a microphone in hand, putting on my own show. I could already tell that everyone in the group was sort of doing their own thing, some of them proudly wearing the Timbiriche T-shirt, and others, like me, wanting to spread their wings and—why not?—try to fly on their own. And just like that, around the same time Capetillo and I left the group, with a mix of pain and sadness, but at the same time excitement for the dreams of 1989.

Around that time I was offered another part on a soap called *Luz y Sombra* (Light and Shadow), which was really more shadow than light, since the script didn't fare too well with the tastes of the audience. But it gave me the chance to meet and work with Enrique Álvarez Félix, and develop a beautiful friendship with his mother, María Félix, La Doña, one of the grand divas of Mexico's golden age of cinema. Her tips and advice helped me a lot. She would always say to me, "Thalia, one's appearance starts at one's feet," and what she meant was that even the manner in which you walk and your posture determine the extent of your grace and personality.

Dream of Being a Soloist

Even as I worked and worked to advance in the world of soap operas, growing and developing as an actress, that crazy surge of work that I did with the group, singing live onstage, was beginning to accumulate into excess energy that I could no longer channel now that I had ceased to be a part of the group. The desire to sing became an unquenchable thirst to launch a career as a solo artist. What I wanted most was to get up onstage and grab the microphone, but I knew that I had to have a plan, some preparation. My dream was beginning to unfold, a dream that I yearned to crystallize: I wanted to be a soloist. I envisioned myself singing my own songs, me alone with the audience, a magical moment shared by us. But to live my dreams I had to make a change, which was why I decided that after the season of *Luz y Sombra* ended, I would move to Los Angeles for a while to study singing and dance. I wanted to learn how to play certain instruments, like the bass guitar, and to work on perfecting my songwriting skills.

So with my dreams in tow, at the ripe young age of seventeen I arrived in Hollywood, accompanied by my inseparable accomplice: my mother. And like my song says: *"playa, sol y palmeras"* ("beach, sun and palm trees")—California, here I am! I rented an apartment in Westwood, where there were nearby movie theaters, restaurants, shops, and cafés—an area that was very young, and perfect for me, since UCLA was also right nearby. What a place! UCLA is one of the top universities in the state of California, and walking through its perfectly manicured campus and seeing the different architectural styles of the buildings, and the young students in groups moving from one end of the campus to the other, was for me an incomparable experience. I took English classes at UCLA, but I also wanted to master an instrument, so I went to the Melrose area, where I wound up taking bass lessons. I would spend my days rushing from one place to the next, since I had my dance classes in Santa Monica, and then I had to drive all the way to the San Fernando Valley for my singing lessons. I would spend my day cruising in my red convertible and blasting music by Aerosmith, Janet Jackson, Madonna, the Doors and Journey.

And through all of this, my mother was like an appendage. She was always attached to me, watching, listening and smelling everything that came before me, to the point that she would even wait for me at the university cafeteria until I finished my classes. It was a bit bizarre to see a woman surrounded by young people, spending hours each day waiting for her youngest daughter to get out of class. It was a very difficult situation for me, because in her desire to take care of me, she compromised my ability to develop independently as a teenager and as a woman. But everything happens for a reason, and if it hadn't been that way, I may not have lived through everything that I did. She did it because she felt that as a mother that was just what she needed to do: protect me. And for that, I will always be grateful.

This adventure in Los Angeles lasted approximately one year, a year in which I disconnected from everyone and everything, a year for me to focus solely on my development as an artist. When I left Timbiriche, Mr. Azcárraga thought that it would be important to give me the opportunity to hone myself, like a diamond in the rough, with regard to acting as well as music. He was my Pygmalion; part of his plan was to send me to study at the center for show business: Los Angeles, California.

Mr. Emilio Azcárraga Milmo, nicknamed "the Tiger," was one of the most influential businessmen nationally and internationally, and was the son of Emilio Azcárraga Vidaurreta, who founded what is today Televisa. Azcárraga Jr. was the owner of Univision and president of the Spanish-language network Galavision.

"The Tiger" was the person who structured the plan of what I needed to learn and refine in order to advance in my career. The main point of my trip to Los Angeles was to develop ideas for my first album as a solo artist; I had to find the tone of my voice, my musical style, the image and general concept of what I wanted to present to the people in an innovative manner, using my ideas and the instinct and taste of the producer Alfredo Díaz Ordaz, who was in charge of the music department of Televisa. Alfredo was an extraordinary genius, an eccentric and a visionary. Since the day we met, we were kindred spirits, and together we were able to create what later became eighties classics such as *"Saliva, Sudor, Sangre"* ("Saliva, Sweat, Blood") and *"Un Pacto Entre los Dos"* ("A Pact Between Us")—songs that marked an era and that today are considered iconic Mexican pop. Destiny brought the two of us together and it was magically explosive.

Back then, singing about secretions in lyrics such as "Your saliva intoxicates me; come here and sweat with me" and, even worse, sadomasochistic themes such as the ones described in *"Un Pacto Entre los Dos"* sparked a huge controversy. And add that to my determination to revive the "flower power" trend, which was the symbol of youthful independence that came out of the sixties. The truth is that my entire being longed to break from anything traditional; I wanted to express myself in my own way, and to find my own voice. It is also possible that somehow, unconsciously, I wanted to break the invisible chains that my mother had locked me in out of love, as did the career where I had left my childhood and part of my adolescence that yearned and screamed for its freedom.

But I was not going to be able to break from traditions on my own, even though I was young and felt all these things inside. With all the living energy that always sought some form of expression, I needed someone to help me channel it the right way. I needed a compadre who thought like me. I found that in my Alfredo, who immediately became my ally, because ever since childhood, he himself had always been a "rebel with a cause." It's funny how certain paths cross in life, but who would have thought that our parents had met at a certain interview on November 18, 1970, Alfredo's father being the president of the Mexican Republic, and my father his interviewer? Who would have imagined that we were so close to each other at a party that my parents were invited to—my mother pregnant with me, and Alfredo, a hyperactive child on the brink of adolescence, running all over the place, turning his parents' party on its head? And last, who would have imagined that at that particular moment in time, each of us with the echoes of our thoughts that finally crystallized as cadenced music, we would work on our own "pact between us"?

Still, being in Los Angeles, I did my homework to look for whatever was necessary for my image, and I found everything that I needed in a little store that was hidden in Melrose. The whole store had a flower-power style, hippie-ism in its fullest expression. I loved it right away, because that was my exact look at the time. That was the door that opened me up to everything that had to do with looks, costumes, innovation and trying the most bizarre things, such as appearing at an awards show wearing a white jacket studded with teddy bears, or a bra made of chrome with two water faucets on the front for my video for *"Piel Morena"* ("Dark Skin"), or the bustier that shot flames for my video for *"Gracias a Dios"* ("Thanks to God"). I experimented with everything: the flower girl, the femme fatale, costumes made of CDs, and different characterizations, such as the Aztec, the Japanese, the Egyptian—and while we're on the subject of bizarre costumes, how about the bra detailed with two small guitars and a headpiece that was reminiscent of a traditional Mexican hat? At the time my looks were very unique, versions of which we see today on great artists like Lady Gaga. Who would have thought that this little store would open up such a Pandora's box? There I bought countless hip-hugger bell-bottom pants, bras and demitops full of flowers and platform shoes, among many other things.

When it was finally time to return to Mexico, I felt superready and sure of myself; I was proud of my experiences and everything I had accomplished. I had learned a lot in my singing and dance lessons, and I felt full of a certain power and freedom that

I had never before tasted. I felt that I was in the right place at the right time, doing exactly what I was destined to do . . . but, surprise, in the end reality hit me quite hard.

My new image, which made me feel confident and totally gratified, was completely different from the little fifteen-year-old girl in pigtails, with bangs in the front and a sweet smile, who played the lead in *Quinceañera*. I suppose that people had gotten used to expecting that from me, and when I returned from Los Angeles with my first album as a solo artist and a totally different image, strong and sensual, I received a lot of harsh criticism, none of which I was prepared for.

The debut of my first solo album, self-titled *Thalia*, was not exactly what I had imagined, even though my record label worked as hard as they could to promote it. The first single from the album, "*Un Pacto Entre los Dos*," was banned by more than half of the most important radio stations in Mexico, since its content was deemed too graphic for their listeners. Words and phrases such as "*Róbalo, amárralo, pégale . . . goza su dolor. Muerdelo, lastimalo, castigalo . . . comparte su pasión*" ("Steal him, tie him up, hit him . . . enjoy the pain. Bite him, hurt him, punish him . . . share the passion") were simply too much for the Mexican audiences of the time, because it's one thing to think these thoughts or to speak of it with friends, but it's something else entirely to launch it into the world as a love song. Besides, just like Sandy in *Grease*, I, too, was evolving from being a sweet young thing into a sensual vixen, and people didn't like that one bit. Nothing was left of that innocent little girl who played Beatriz on *Quinceañera*; and in her place was an eighteen-year-old girl in skintight bell-bottom pants with huge flowers. You could see my midriff, because I wore only a floral demibra on top. I liked the look a lot, but more than anything I adopted it because I wanted to do something different, something with a provocative lure for my audience, something that the people would want to follow. I even painted a blond streak on the front part of my hair. That's how I came out to sing my first single, "*Un Pacto Entre los Dos.*"

I had no idea what awaited me.

Obviously, none of this went over well with the conservative society of my country at that time. They all asked themselves, "What happened to the girl in the pigtails? How vulgar!" I got the sense that the people felt let down and wondered how it was possible that I didn't have someone managing my image. The public said all sorts of nasty things to me! The comments came down like hail: "And she claims to be an icon for the young?" the critics asked. "In her dreams!"

Back then, no one in my community went out dressed like that, which was precisely why I wanted so badly to break with the norm, with that image of the good girl that we young artists had to keep up so ardently in order to get ahead. Of course, there were already stars who came out onstage looking "provocative," such as Alejandra Guzman, a true rocker, pure dynamite onstage, and with a vocal sound that was so seductive and sensual that it immediately won the favor of the young fans. There was also Gloria Trevi, with her irreverent lyrics; she deconstructed the canons of social norms and forged a movement of young people who could express themselves freely through her songs. But in my case—having been a part of a group as important and adored as Timbiriche, in which people watched me grow up, and having been an actor on television who resonated with so many little girls of that time—my image change was way more obvious to the public, and a lot more difficult and challenging for them to assimilate.

Despite all the hard work and effort that I put into recording and promoting my first album, reviewers continued to be implacable. This reaction hit me very hard, and I had a moment of extreme doubt, pain and shame. I felt that my world was crumbling to pieces; there seemed to be no way out; there was no way to explain myself. . . . There was nothing . . . only the humiliation that came with my shattered dreams and my heartache. In fact, I got to a point where I just threw myself onto my bed and cried and didn't leave my room for two weeks. I didn't even want to see the sun, and did not allow my mother to open the shades.

My mother gave me some time to work through my pain, but one day, tired of seeing me cry inconsolably, she walked into my room and opened the blinds all the way and said, "Okay, honey, you are eighteen years old, you are talented, intelligent—and besides, you have a fabulous figure; you don't look vulgar in the least bit. Come on; don't go on like this. Get up, and keep moving forward." And all I could do was tell her that I had done everything from the bottom of my heart, and that I couldn't understand how people could be so malicious and attack me so ruthlessly. I showed her my hands, which were all calloused from manually attaching the flowers to my costume. How could the whole heart and soul of the album be judged by just one song? How could they end the life span of an album after hearing just one single?

Perhaps I didn't appreciate at the time that my mother knew better than anyone the great effort and the hard work that was involved in making my dreams a reality. She knew because she was right there with me from the beginning and never stopped believing in me. In addition to being my mother, she was my manager, and the first person to support my wearing those clothes in order to break with the norm and to try to be different. She was the one who motivated me to try something daring and innovative, something that would express all of that energy that had built up in me. Never, not even once, did she stop supporting me in doing everything that I dreamed of.

To snap me out of my depression as quickly as possible, my mother laid out my options: "Look, honey," she said, "we could keep beating ourselves up over the negative reviews about your album and your new image as a solo artist, plunge into this disastrous depression, and it's over; your career is finished and this is as far as you got. You can dedicate yourself to something else, like biology or psychology, which you always loved so much as a little girl."

I lay on the bed thinking, *How could it be that this is as far as I got?* while she continued talking: "Now, if you want to continue with your career and you want to leave Mexico, let's pack up our bags, close up the house, and travel the world to start from scratch somewhere else. You have Spain, Italy; there are literally thousands of places and tons of opportunities. . . ." She paused briefly and looked me in the eyes: "But if you want to stay in Mexico and continue with your profession, just as you had desired and dreamed, then get out of that bed and go defend your talent like a lioness. . . . Do you hear me?"

I thought about what she said and realized that she was totally right. I could not let myself be brought down. I was simply not going to allow it to happen. In the end, my mother added, one day we would both laugh about all the things that she had just said.

"My love," she said, "what doesn't kill you will make you stronger. You'll see how you will come out of this even fiercer and more powerful."

If we could have seen what awaited me in the near future—that I would achieve gold albums, that four of my singles would come to be iconic songs that accompanied a whole generation and continue to stir the collective nostalgia of so many—if I had seen that, I would have known that my mother was right. Totally right. I would either have to run away from the whole thing, or I would have to endure it like a warrior, and, well . . . I endured, and it was all well worth it.

That day I learned one of the most valuable lessons that my mother ever taught me: I learned that one's worth is carried within and that sometimes we need to face situations head-on, no matter how painful they may be, because it is the only way to become stronger, wiser and more human.

Onward and Upward

There's a saying that when God squeezes you by the neck, He doesn't choke—and even though the media's initial reaction might have hit me hard, I kept moving forward. In 1991 I released my second album, entitled *Mundo de Cristal* (*Crystal World*), with plenty of controversial tracks, such as "*Sudor*" ("Sweat"), "*Fuego Cruzado*" ("Crossfire") and "*En la Intimidad*" ("In Intimacy"). Then an opportunity came up in Spain: I was offered the job of cohost on a variety show on the Telecinco network called *VIP Noche* (*VIP Night*) in its three formats: *El Show VIP*, *VIP Noche* and *VIP Guay*. So I quickly packed my bags, and off we went on this new adventure. I sang and danced on the show, particularly in tributes to famous films such as *Pretty Woman, The Little Mermaid, 9½ Weeks, Flashdance* and *Dirty Dancing*, among many more. I'd dress up in character and perform one of the main songs from the film in Spanish, with lavish costumes and over-the-top routines. I had the good fortune to work with the conductor Emilio Aragón, who was already a great Spanish icon. We had an absolute blast. From the moment I landed on the show, I felt right at home, because once there I was able to tap into a very free and creative way of thinking. I adapted right away to my work and became friends with everyone. From the very first rehearsal with the Italian choreographer, practicing with thirty other dancers who were in each show, and even memorizing my lines, I felt so at ease. Spain for me was the motherland, and to this day I fondly remember the instant acceptance that the public gave me, and that I continue to feel today whenever I step foot on the Iberian Peninsula.

We spent almost one whole year living in Madrid, and I can honestly say that every single day that I spent there was extraordinary. Gradually, in that enjoyable, fun and friendly atmosphere, I was able to recoup my self-confidence, until I got to a point where I felt more than ready to take on any project, to fully immerse myself in anything that I wanted. I had so much energy that while I worked on the television program, I recorded my third album, called *Love,* which included "*Sangre*" ("Blood"), "Love," "*La Vie en Rose,*" "*Cien Años*" ("One Hundred Years") and "*Flor de Juventud*" ("Flower of Youth").

One simple phone call would change my life in a matter of forty-eight hours. One day my mother and I were resting in the hotel when the phone suddenly rang. It was Valentin Pimstein. My heart started to race, because I knew that even just hearing his voice could be a prelude to great things.

Perhaps few people know who he is outside of Mexico, but Valentin Pimstein is a well-known producer of soap operas. He was the man who produced the soaps starring Verónica Castro, Lucía Méndez, Edith González, Leticia Calderón and Victoria Ruffo, some of the best soap opera actresses of the time—soaps such as *Simplemente María* (*Simply Maria*), *Carrusel* (*Carousel*),

Rosa Salvaje (*Savage Rose*), *Monte Calvario* (*Cavalry Mountain*), *Vivir un Poco* (*Live a Little*), and the eighties classic *Amalia Batista*. Valentin Pimstein was the king of the melodrama genre at the time, kind of like a Mexican Aaron Spelling, the great visionary of soaps . . . a King Midas who turned me into a Queen Midas.

He called me from his offices in Mexico to tell me that he had a script for a soap opera in hand that was about to begin filming, and that I was the only person who could possibly star. Apparently a lot of people had already auditioned, but nobody seemed right for the part. He told me that he wanted me to play the role of María Mercedes, because he had tried out a few actresses, but what he really wanted was a fresh face, someone young. He was convinced that he needed a new face, and he was certain that that face was mine. As you can imagine, my mother and I could not contain our emotions, and like two little girls we jumped up and down on the bed. And why wouldn't we? It was as if someone had just handed me a winning lottery ticket. Amazingly, the dates of shooting the series coincided with the last days of my time with *VIP Noche*, so without any issues or sense of remorse, with a once-in-a-lifetime proposition in hand and my mind full of hopes and dreams, I returned to my beloved country.

The Marías Trilogy

The project proposed by Pimstein was very interesting, and was like a rewrite of *Rosa Salvaje*, which at the time featured wonderful actors. The role being offered to me had been played by Verónica Castro, the Mexican actress who cracked the international market for Mexico. Now, the same producer that had turned Verónica Castro into a megastar was calling *me* for that part! Wow! I couldn't believe it. I was going to be María Mercedes. And because I was in the process of wrapping up my third album, *Love,* he even decided that one of my songs would be integrated into the María Mercedes theme song, so in one shot I was the star of a new soap opera and had a new record out.

Welcome back to Mexico!

To film the soap opera, I gave my heart and soul. I had to study all kinds of things, from the current Mexican slang to juggling to the market in Tepito, where I could study the correct dialect and physical nuances of expression. In doing so, I was layering my character with personality. The show did wonderfully both nationally and internationally; the success was so great—and this was just one of hundreds of stories reported in the press— that in Vietnam, the night they aired the finale, the episode that would divulge the outcome of the story, a record number of cars were stolen because, in a rush to get home in time to watch the show, people hastily left their cars unlocked. It is likely that even the police officers were glued to their televisions while the thieves did their thing.

I went on with my crazy workload: during the week shooting for the soap, and on weekends I would go to sing in the *palenques,* put on private shows, and do photo shoots for magazines. . . . In sum, the little machine didn't stop. I became a workaholic.

One day during a work meeting, Valentin Pimstein sat next to me, and with a steady voice and that elegant and educated Chilean essence of his that made me feel so good, he said, "Darling, you are going to be the star of the first soap opera trilogy that has ever existed in the history of television. I already have your next two projects lined up, and we will call them the Marías Trilogy." He spoke to me with great affection. "You will see, dear; you will be the Pedrito Infante of my productions."

Marimar, the second installment of the trilogy, began in late 1993. Marimar was a role that allowed me to feel totally comfortable. Since my grandfather was from La Paz, Baja California, I had been hearing that coastal singsong dialect my entire life. Even though they gave me a wonderful dialect coach to learn the various tonalities, my real way of practicing was speaking to my grandmother, who was an authentic coastal soul. I lived in the world the soap opera evoked, and the little dresses that they had us wear were like the ones we wore when we used to go to La Paz. I wore my hair natural, since the humidity would make it take its own shape, allowing its own natural curl and bounce. Marimar was for me like a character who grew up right at home with me; she was part of my roots; she was real, which was just how I projected her, and which is why I believe people so immediately connected with the character. The viewers felt compassion and love for the beach girl, and it was that simple girl who spoke multiple dialects and cultures, until she was able to speak one collective language—the language of hope and light at the end of the tunnel. That's how Marimar was accepted by millions of souls all over the world. The soap aired in 180 countries, was translated into every language on the planet, and took me to places that I could have never imagined.

The trilogy closed with *María la del Barrio* (*Maria from the Neighborhood*), and was a huge success in Mexico. I sang the title song on my fourth album, *En Éxtasis* (*In Ecstasy*), which was released in 1995. (The album also contained my hit *"Piel Morena,"* produced by Emilio Estefan.) This fusion launched me to unparalleled international stardom. Contracts and invitations seemed to rain down on me, I did all kinds of shows and private concerts, I performed at the Viña del Mar International Song Festival, and I went on promotional tours in the United States. There was a perfect balance in my career as a singer and actress, and they fed each other mutually.

Over two billion people worldwide watched the trilogy of Marías. Together with the three Marías, my music was able to reach so many different parts of the globe; people sought out the title songs from the soaps, which were strategically included on my latest album, and my songs were promoted along with each soap opera. The public bought my albums, and my songs became known all over the world.

The day I realized that I was able to break new frontiers with my music, I felt professionally accomplished. My international success has been one of the most important milestones of my career. I traveled a lot; I got to visit many different countries and incredible people; I saw the world in a manner that I could have never dreamed. It was not just the honor of being paid for doing my show, but whenever I arrived anywhere, I was treated like royalty; even the press in some of these countries referred to me as the Aztec queen, the Mexican queen, or the ambassador of Mexico, and like a proud peacock, I always brought my country's flag with me wherever I went to represent my motherland. I was in the clouds at the pinnacle of my career.

When I arrived in Manila, for example, the president of the Philippines welcomed me as if I were a head of state. I accompanied him to a groundbreaking event at a new residential complex, met with the press, reviewed a formation of soldiers who were impeccably uniformed, and placed a traditional crown of flowers at the monument to their national heroes. I visited schools, orphanages and nurseries. I found out later that there was a countdown to my arrival on national television: "Just one more week . . . just three days . . . just two days left . . . just a couple of hours until the arrival of Thalia, Marimar, María *la del barrio.*" And when I arrived there were so many people at the airport that cars could not get through. It was amazing. The streets were packed on both sides, with people yelling, "Maria! . . . Marimar! María *la del barrio!*" I'd see hundreds of smiling faces, screaming or in some cases crying. They would wave their arms at me, and hold up posters of me in character or signs with different phrases accompanied by hearts. Wherever I went, rivers of people would always follow.

One day, on the bus en route to a performance in the auditorium at noon, I suddenly saw throngs of people in motion—a mass of humans.

"What's happening?" my mother and I asked nervously. "It looks like a state of siege, and with the helicopter hovering there . . ."

We really did become very nervous, and for a moment we thought we had been caught in the middle of a revolution, but the organizers calmed us down: "Thalia, it's the people who want to see you . . . and the helicopter up there is covering every step that you take live on television. Don't worry," they said. My mother and I looked at each other, and they added, "The last time something like this happened was when Pope John Paul the Second came to visit on January fourteenth, 1995."

I didn't believe it and only raised my hand to give a wave.

Like everyone, I wanted to go out and explore the magnificent places I visited, but I had an experience that really helped to serve as a warning. I wanted to get some typical Philippine costumes to wear, so one day we went to a mall, and in one of the stores my mother, sisters and I almost bought the entire store—not just the costumes, but also some beautiful fabrics so that we could order custom-made dresses. That was what we were doing when suddenly we began to hear screams. They became louder and louder, so we went to see what was happening. The authorities had closed off the area that we were in, and since word had spread that I was there, we saw that people were pounding on the glass windows that served as doors, to the point that we had to exit through the building's "entrails." The people even shook the store windows, and almost shattered them to pieces.

From that moment on, we devised a strategy so that I would be able to actually stroll through the places we visited. In one city in the Philippines I wore a long dress and covered my face—with just my eyes showing—as was the tradition of women in that region. To not arouse suspicions I told my bodyguard, who was a big guy, to walk right in front of me, as if I were his wife. That was how we arrived at the popular market, where I wanted to buy everything, as there were so many beautiful and unique things that I was totally enthralled. But when I went to pay for one of the objects—with a fish-scale pattern that I liked—the woman looked at my eyes and signaled with her index finger. "You are Marimar . . . Marimar. . . ." All I could make out was "Marimar," and before I had time to make sense of what was happening, my bodyguard had already picked me up and I found myself in the car that was speeding away from the market. How could she possibly recognize me behind the veil? I will never know.

Some news stations did a report on record-setting audience sizes and announced that in the Philippines, the country that probably felt the greatest social impact from *Marimar,* the show was more widely promoted than the 1998 World Cup and more highly rated than the Super Bowl or the Grammys. In fact, while I was visiting the country, the people and the media were so enthralled to see Marimar in the flesh that a historic peace treaty between the government and the guerillas and the centennial celebrations of the Philippine Revolutions that were happening at the same time were pushed aside in the midst of Marimar fever. As a result, the archipelago was temporarily dubbed "*Republica de Mari Mar.*"

I accepted every invitation that came to me from the Philippines. How could I say no, considering that this country had given me so much? The problem was that I didn't know that all of these honors also hid political agendas. Somehow, the government was using my visit to win the favor of the people. Gradually, I became aware of it and started to become more informed, because the last thing I wanted was for them to use me to gain votes, and then have the Filipinos think that I was backing one candidate over another. I am an artist and I have never wanted to involve myself in the politics of a country—certainly not when I don't know enough background to be able to form my own ideas.

At the time, Imelda Marcos, wife of the late ex-president Ferdinand Marcos, was in the midst of a presidential campaign, and she invited me to a dinner so that she could meet me. She had a whole dinner prepared for me; however, knowing the history of Marcos and the people and the delicate situation of the country, with lots of care and courtesy I declined the invitation, and sent a nice letter saying that I would not be able to attend. With everything that she and her husband had done, it was impossible for me to accept that invitation. If my fans were to see me photographed with her, it would be sure to hurt someone's feelings.

Because of my great success there, I decided to record an album, which was titled *Nandito Ako*, that was launched exclusively in the Philippines, of which the first track was "*Nandito Ako.*" This was the first time that I learned a new language, in this case Tagalog, for the sole purpose of recording an album, although it was accompanied by other songs in English. Just one week after the record was released, I earned a platinum record.

Every country surprised me more than the last. One of those places was Indonesia. What an interesting place! I loved its people, its culture, its food, its music and, most of all, its dance. I wanted to take Indonesian dance classes; I marveled at the perfection of their movements, the lack of expression on their faces, which were practically blank, making them look like giant marionettes that showed no emotion—they opened their eyes in such a way that they appeared to come out of their sockets. The movements of their bodies were mathematic; they looked like sculptures that had come out of one of their temples and come to life.

After that trip, I began to incorporate some of those movements into my choreography. On a day when I wasn't working in Bali, I went to visit some of the most popular little villages, and in one of them the rice plantation workers invited me to their homes and served me a plate of rice that they had just harvested that afternoon, while a group of musicians practiced nearby. Seeing me so excited, they taught me how to play in a *gamelan,* a musical ensemble that features a variety of instruments.

I always think that they honestly thought I was Marimar, and not Thalia, because the sensation that the soap created in Asia was unparalleled. The Asian public was obsessed with the sweet beach girl. I thought it was so lovely to see their faces all lit up when I would sit at their tables, eating with them, as if it was a scene in the soap opera and they were actually dining with Marimar. They practically looked for Marimar's dog, Pulgoso, to see if I had brought him with me. I could feel their pride in being able to share a few minutes of their lives with me, and that filled my heart. Some of the women were so worked up they even cried. The Marimar phenomenon was unexplainable, a whirlwind of experiences and emotions that impacted me profoundly. I would spend a whole day at the table with the villagers, and the next day I would sit at the table with the governor, being honored with a lavish feast with the elite of the country, dozens of local musicians and never-ending banquets of food. It was a fantastic welcoming. A special gown was sent to my hotel. It was tailored to my size, made of the finest silks in the land and embroidered with gold. After being in the village with the rice musicians, which was what I affectionately called them, I would go on to spend time with some of the best musicians in the country, all of them dressed in their best silk finery.

I still get excited when I think about those amazing times. Soap operas made a lot of history; just look at the report by UNESCO, where it was noted that "in the Ivory Coast in Africa and in Paris people stopped the daily course of their lives" to watch a soap opera. I never expected that kind of success.

From the moment we landed at an airport, regardless of where we were, there were fans already waiting for me in their cars, and they would accompany me all the way to my hotel. They would make giant cards, and would resourcefully put multiple sheets of paper together, and then they would roll the whole thing up like giant toilet paper; there were meters and meters of "Thalia, I love you." They would bombard me with teddy bears, flowers, hearts, and cards smacked with kisses; and this would happen not only all over South America, but also in places like Greece, Hungary and so many other cities in Europe. I was warmly received in both the Old and New Worlds. For example, in Brazil, where I would appear live on shows, I was always amazed when the girls saw me and would cup their faces with their hands, grabbing their own cheeks, and screaming and crying with all of their might.

Sometimes at my hotel, I would look out the window and see

fans sleeping on the ground the night before a concert, waiting for me so that they could say hi. In those cases, I would send someone from my crew to get them something to eat and to tell them that it made me very nervous to see them lying there, to please go home and sleep in their own houses that night, promising that I would greet them the next day. This happened to me a lot on tours, because when we did the shows, members of my fan clubs would follow us, which was totally fine by me as long as they would allow me to pay for hotel rooms so that they wouldn't spend the night sleeping on the streets. I was always determined to take care of my fans, because they take care of me. They are my people, my friends, and they are the most loyal followers. A lot of these fan clubs still exist, and they've been with me since the beginning. In time, a lot of the female members of the fan clubs had children, and they have even named their babies after me, and their little daughters know my songs. My prize—my reward for so much hard work.

Wherever I was, entire families would gather and speak to me in their native tongues, while still singing my songs in Spanish. It was so crazy! In Brazil they crowned me queen of carnival of a samba school in Rio de Janeiro, which was without a doubt one of the most amazing experiences of my life. Besides, I fell hopelessly in love with Rio de Janeiro, its food, its music and its zest for life, all of which planted the idea in my mind to record an album in Portuguese for that market.

The last soap opera I did was *Rosalinda,* with a script by Delia Fiallo, and produced by Salvador Mejía. The show debuted in 1999, and despite the fact that it didn't rate as high as the Marías, it was still a great success. In places like Peru, Argentina, Bolivia, Holland, France, the United States, Germany and Africa, it was a tremendous hit.

But by then, my health was starting to become compromised; we were working very intensely. I remember one time when we had to film a scene at an old roller coaster and the lights for the scene were missing. My day had started at seven in the morning; it was already three a.m. and the lights were still not there. I couldn't sit or lie down to rest, since I couldn't wrinkle the costume; all I could do was recline on a sort of handrail. We finally starting filming at around four in the morning; it was minus four degrees, and I was barely wearing any clothes. It was so horribly cold I couldn't feel my toes. When we finally finished, I had spent twenty-four hours straight shooting. How was I not going to get sick? I had a cold and a fever that lasted a whole week, but no matter what, I couldn't stop working.

Gypsy Life

Very early on in my career, from the moment my mother and I went to live in Los Angeles, our life took on a sort of Gypsy vibe. We would go on trips for long stretches at a time, when we would live in hotel rooms, schlepping luggage from one place to the next. We would return home maybe three times a year, at the most. We didn't stop. It was a lifestyle that I adored, because every day a new and fascinating experience awaited us, and as far as that was concerned, I was never bored. My mother and I lived happily, but my sisters longed to have their mother back for special occasions, during hard times, or just on a regular Sunday afternoon. My mother's attention was focused on me for many years, when in reality she had four other daughters who loved her and needed her as much as I did. But without our intending it, things just worked out this way.

My sisters often thought that my mother favored me and they

had stopped existing for her. That, of course, was not true, but that was how they felt, and I have to admit that to a certain point, I understood their feelings What they wanted in the deepest parts of their souls was a mother who was present, and maybe because of that, they didn't understand how we could live so submerged in my career, and that we had allowed work to consume us to the point that we no longer spent time as a family, like old times.

If we weren't on the phone confirming financial arrangements, or discussing a new role on a soap, we were resolving issues with the team of accountants, lawyers, or other individuals who were involved with our projects. I remember on one Mother's Day we were at the house of one of my sisters when we got a phone call saying that my sound engineer and bandleader were in jail in a South American country, because they'd arrived without me and no one believed that they were there to do a show. I had already paid for the costs of the show, and the team had gone early to get things ready for my arrival. We tried to resolve the matter by phone, but it was impossible, so we had to leave the whole family gathered together and get on an emergency flight to go deal with the issue. The truth is that our lives were pretty hectic, and it was hard to explain to our loved ones.

In Mexico, there are an infinite number of festivals held in honor of spring, with the livestock and customs of each place, village or region—and, of course, the *palenque* is never missing. The *palenque* is a stage like a miniature bullfighting ring, with various rows of wooden benches and stools placed around the circle, where both the most important artists play and the notorious cockfights take place. It's safe to say that the majority of Mexican artists have all passed through *palenques,* and I always found performing there the hardest, because you had to wait for the cockfights to finish so that the stage could be cleaned off, the instruments plugged in and the sound check done for the show. This could be anywhere from twelve midnight until two in the morning, depending on how long it took the losing rooster to die! There is an entire underworld economy that goes along with those shows, and everything is paid in cash. One time, my mother got into an argument with a *palenque* owner who was like a Mafia type, and she said to him, "If you don't pay us up front, Thalia doesn't sing." And the guy drew his gun and pointed it right at my mother's chest and answered, "You sure she won't sing, sweetheart?" Needless to say, the show started three minutes later.

We didn't share these experiences with my sisters, because we didn't want to worry them. They saw only what everybody else saw; it was easier for them to find out about things by way of the news than from the two of us, who were always so busy that we never really had the time to sit and talk about the experiences we were having. Maybe that was why it was hard for them to really understand our day-to-day lives. We were living in two different realities. While they had time to hang out with their friends and attend events for their kids, I was running at a million miles per hour, with my mother always by my side.

It's hard to describe the amount of work that is involved in a career like this when fame and success have come knocking at your door. Sometimes you find yourself swimming in a hurricane of projects, jobs, different personas and pressures—essentially living in a whirlwind where time does not exist; it goes like water, and suddenly you don't even know where you are. You wake up in one hotel and fall asleep in another one; you get on a plane and fly twelve hours to arrive at your destination, and with no glamour whatsoever you trek the interminable terminals in various airports, just to make your connection to the next country. Your fans say farewell in one language, and new ones welcome you in another; you don't eat well because you have time only to bolt down whatever is quickly and easily within your reach; you lose hours of sleep, hours of time with your loved ones, hours, days and months of your life. The producers want you to perform on their show and everyone wants to have something to do with you; they want a piece of you, a little chunk of you. When they look at you, they see dollar signs, and you can practically see what they are thinking: *She is going to make our year.* You start charging more money for new work, and that number starts to increase all the time. Fame kicks into action, and in that moment the public, the fans, somehow become a primordial part of your life, because it is really they who are keeping you at the top.

When I was back home, my sisters would call me, and we would go out for lunch or dinner, or we would get together to watch movies in one of their homes, but I was so tired that I would fall asleep on the couch, waking up only to say good-bye and go home. On other occasions I was so immersed in my own little world, so obsessed with my career, that I was not conscious of the fact that the people my sisters were looking for were my mother and their younger sister, and not the manager and the artist.

The fact that my mother had dedicated herself so intensely to my career, I think, has to do with the reality that she herself was a frustrated actress who never got to live out her dream. When she was very young, my mother was such an exceptionally beautiful woman that people would turn around and stare when she walked down the street. She had the kind of beauty of actresses from the golden age of Hollywood, like Rita Hayworth, and with such a magnificent body for a girl of just fifteen. That was why she was pursued by the boys of the neighborhood where she lived, and by the most influential men, too. That was the case, for example, with Emilio Fernández, best known as "El Indio" Fernández, a great producer and filmmaker of Mexico's golden age of cinema, who spotted my mother and immediately followed her and handed her a business card inviting her to go to the Churubusco Studios for auditions. These studios were very famous in the mid-fifties; they were like our Mexican Hollywood. It was the place where black-and-white films were screened on reels; the place where Mexican cinema truly evolved. But my mother never went.

Another time, a man who lived near her house invited her to appear on a show called *Variedades de Medio Día* (*Daytime Varieties*). My mom told us that people would always come by and ask my grandmother for permission to photograph her daughter, and my grandmother always said the same thing: "No, no and no!" which left my mother with a type of unsatisfied feeling about what could have been. She never got to be an actress, but she was undoubtedly able to experience the whole process vicariously through me, and she developed into a wonderful businesswoman; maybe she wasn't in front of the cameras, as she had once desired in her heart, but she was the face behind the cameras, which gave her a lot of strength.

When fame takes you over with all of its glory, when everybody loves you, when everyone sings your songs, when executives fight over you and pay you double or triple so that you show up at this or that place, and they send private jets for you filled with everything you want, it is very easy to lose perspective. Your feet start to disconnect from the ground and you are not really aware of what is going on, because everything feels like a dream.

Fame takes you out of your reality and puts you on a jet where everything is possible; and sometimes that feeling of power made me do stupid and arrogant things for the simple sake of doing them. One night when I was on tour in Spain, while we had some time off to have fun, I went to a club with my dancers and musicians, who were my only friends at the time. We sat in a private VIP area and the bottles of champagne started coming. I sat on the sofa, and there were lots of handsome men around with drinks, looking at me and flirting. One of my friends said, "You are so silly, Thalia! Haven't you noticed that guy over there looking at you, and that he is gorgeous? If I were you, I would be standing over there talking to him."

To which my ego from that era responded, "Haven't you noticed that I get what I want when I want it? Watch me snap my fingers and he'll come over here like a slaughtered lamb."

And that was what I basically did. I looked right at him and beckoned with my index finger for him to come over, and the poor guy came over to meet me. He was the hottest guy in the room, and he walked over with a great big smile to sit beside me. When he sat down, I turned to my friend and, sure of what I had done, said, "Satisfied? Whatever I want, I get, and if I want to take this guy somewhere else, I'll take him. And if I want to buy him, I can do that, too."

I think about it now and I cannot believe that I was capable of saying such things. At that point, I was only around twenty-three or twenty-four years old, and I already felt like a goddess. I thought that the world was at my fingertips and that I could control everything and everyone around me. . . . I was completely unaware how little control any of us have over the world and how fragile our lives can be. At the time I was used to everything always going my way, and when it didn't, I would instantly get annoyed, and it would affect me in the deepest part of my being.

There was one occasion in particular when I remember feeling a blow to the ego. I had spent two years dating a certain boyfriend, one of the young businessmen who were at the forefront of society back then. In my world, we had the perfect relationship: two young successful people who liked to enjoy themselves. But one day he decided to stop calling me for no apparent reason. This surprised me so much, and I took it as a personal offense. Nobody left Thalia! Quite the contrary—it was Thalia who sent people flying!

I decided to go out for dinner with my friends to a restaurant in the city, and I was shocked when, as I walked into the place, I spotted him putting a coat on a girl to walk out of the very same door that I was walking into. When I saw him, I was paralyzed. I didn't know what to do, whether to pull him over and talk to him, to slander him, or to throw it around Maria Felix style (the greatest Mexican actress of all time), looking him up and down as if he were nothing. The truth is that I stood there like a plant, and like that, "planted," I let my friends take me over to the bar. With no hesitation, they ordered five rounds of tequila shots. As I drank my shots, I thought back on all the times I'd done the same thing as my ex had just done to me: My strategy was that when a relationship no longer did it for me, I would gently hint, indirectly, that we should separate and each go our own way. Most of the time the man didn't want to hear it and would play dumb, going on with the relationship as if nothing had happened, and I would think, *There is no blinder person than the one who doesn't want to see. He who is a masochist knows it until his death.* And with no courtesy whatsoever, I would just go on to another relationship. When the man found out and confronted me, I would say, "Ah, well, I tried to tell you in so many ways, but you wouldn't listen."

That night, sitting with my tequila, I pretty much had a taste of my own medicine. It was such a great lesson that it stirred my feelings of guilt and my need to redeem myself. I felt so bad that

I got hold of all the address books I had filled over the years, and picked up the phone to call each person, one by one, asking for forgiveness for the damages I had done. Some of them said, "What are you talking about? That was more than five years ago. I don't even remember that anymore." Others would confirm, "You don't know how badly I needed to hear that from you. Thank you." It was incredible to hear, "You know what, Thalia? I forgive you," and after I did this, many little pieces of my soul came back to me.

There are moments in life when you are stopped right in your tracks. It is so that you don't continue as you are; these moments need to sit you down or slap you right in the face so that you can reevaluate and wake up revaluing your essence as a human being and realize that not even fame, success or self-regard can give you the peace and love for which this world exists.

Unforgettable Moments

As the years passed by and I lived through a sort of "Queen Midas" era, I profoundly erred on so many occasions. Or the equivalent: I had to ask for forgiveness so many times! It is still difficult for me to look at photos of myself from that time, because after the success of the Marías, I endured three years of unbridled craziness with inhumane work schedules. That is why, when I saw Britney Spears getting divorced and then getting derailed—it hit me really hard and I felt sorry for her, but I understood her completely. Because when you are so young and vulnerable and you don't know anything about life, when all of a sudden everyone is aware of what you are doing and saying, or what your childhood teddy bear's name is . . . you get to a point where you need to rebel. It's your way of telling the fans and press, "You people made me this way—now put up with me; I'm no longer the good girl that you wanted me to be—I have a whole other side." And this turns into a huge conflict that only you can face.

With an excess of power, you feel that you run the whole world. You can do whatever you want, whenever you want, and you actually do it. How many times did I close down entire restaurants to privately dine on extravagant dishes with my family and friends? When I did soap operas, I always had a private gym in my dressing room. This had never been seen before, and not even the most important actresses in the history of Mexican television ever had that. I had a refrigerator, microwave, bed, shower, everything that I needed or asked for. My characters were all dressed in Versace, Moschino, D&G and Escada. To many it probably seemed like limitless extravagance, but the truth is that I lived in those studios for a year and a half, I didn't go out, I never had time to eat out, and I practically did not see the light of day. I had no life. What I didn't realize at the time was what an incredible education I received at Televisa. Working on my music and the telenovelas simultaneously was seriously exhausting but irreplaceable training for a performer. Maybe that is why I always got what I wanted. I had a special menu that was cooked just for me, in the kitchen of the highest executives, and each day, meals were brought to my dressing room, because I didn't even have the energy to walk to the dining room. In fact, I was always choosing: "Either I walk and waste my energy, or I save it for the next twenty-four scenes that we still have to shoot." It was a great investment to be able to achieve this international dream that had been swirling around my mind since I was a little girl.

When I was working in Mexico, sometimes I would go out to try to have some fun with friends, but it was only on special occasions, like when our national soccer team made it to the World Cup and all of Mexico gathered at the Angel statue in downtown Mexico City to celebrate. We all went wearing wrestling masks, to blend in with the millions of fanatics who were celebrating in the streets. We even bought some cans of spray "snow" and we would play hide-and-seek, conducting a little war among us. It was a great surge of mischief that made me feel alive, screaming and having fun like an ordinary person, participating in a moment of national glory.

But moments like those were few and far between. Despite everything I had, in reality I was always locked inside my work. I got used to going into clothing stores, which would close especially for me, and buying myself the latest collection of a designer that I liked. The bags would be taken to the hotel and I would spend the afternoon trying on my new clothes. And why not? I saw it as my payment for working that hard for so many hours and so many years. It was like when you are on a diet all the time and the weekend comes and you have a slice of pizza, chocolate cake with whipped cream and a strawberry milk shake. Sometimes they would reserve a private room for me at some of my favorite restaurants, after I worked seventeen hours locked in a Televisa recording studio. And this created a great air of mystery about what I said or did: from having three of my ribs removed—and kept, according to legend, in formaldehyde by a doctor in his clinic as a reward for his work—to the interminable list of my supposed requirements when I worked: white candles, special flowers, incense from a certain temple in India, bottles of water brought from exotic places . . . in sum, things that never, ever crossed my mind. Unfortunately, people believe what they hear on gossip shows, which is where these types of stories appear. Even today, many times when I am talking or interacting with someone I don't know, they tell me they are surprised to see that I am so normal and authentic. They are surprised at how I am because a lot of articles written about me depict me as someone who is nothing more than plastic or fake. Maybe sometimes that image weighed more heavily than what I was willing to give, and what was portrayed had very little to do with my true self.

But in the middle of all that craziness, the myths, and the hours locked inside the studios, or making full use of my limited free moments, my greatest joy was always when I was able to draw out a smile from another human being. When it was almost Christmas, for example, it was as if I were injected with a new kind of energy, and I began to plan everything to activate my personal projects, such as taking trucks filled with toys to the poorer neighborhoods, or making Christmas baskets filled with everything from turkeys, bread, sausages and all kinds of canned goods, to pastas, rice, grains and first-aid supplies for my entire team. I would also take a truck loaded with teddy bears to an orphanage; it was a way to feel alive, seeing these smiling faces of the kids. That really filled me; it was truly the only thing that nourished my soul at that time.

What did I learn from all this? That success robs you of many things, but it also gives you a lot. I learned that beyond my own expectations and obsessions with perfection, I am a very disciplined person. I have an innate ability to do what I am told I should do, to the best of my ability and in record time, if possible. María Felix once told me that discipline is the most important thing to have in this career. But mine was—and still is—almost beyond that. It is a force that comes from my insides and obligates me to always go the extra mile. I am very dedicated. Anywhere I need to be, I have always gotten there early, ready to rehearse, with hair and makeup ready from dawn when necessary. Sometimes I was even willing to take physical risks to do my work well, and I've got plenty of examples.

In *Marimar*, we did a scene in which I ran away upon finding out that my boyfriend was going to get married. I had to run like mad to the top of a cliff, as if I were going to jump off. It was a real cliff, and the directors offered to use a safety rope, so that there would be no risk of an accident. But without thinking twice, I told them that I would do it just like that, naturally, without ropes or stunt doubles. I wanted the scene to come out as realistically as possible. I always felt the suffering of my characters. I think that is why I became depressed so often when I worked on soaps. My whole body would ache because Sergio broke Marimar's heart, or Jorge Luis de Olmo stood up María Mercedes, simply because she was poor and had no education. All my characters went crazy at some point, and I did, too. When María Mercedes was committed to an asylum, there was a scene in which they tied me up and left me lying in a stark hospital room. That scene was so intense for me that I entered a state of shock in real life, because I had to scream and use so much force with the actors playing the nurses that I think I lost sight of the fact that it was only a scene. I believed it was real. We finished shooting and I could not stop crying; I was totally hysterical for an hour and a half. I had to lock myself in my dressing room. It was like a catharsis, perhaps provoked by the long hours of such hard work.

During *Marimar*, I had to wear a thick coat of makeup every day from head to toe to portray a girl who lived by the beach, with bronze, sun-kissed skin. They used the darkest shade of brown foundation on me. How could I forget that? My skin would dry up and I would get acne because all of my pores were clogged. Each week I had to spend time with an aesthetician, having facials and laser treatments for my acne.

Something else that happened with the beach girl, and which I ultimately took home with me, was the smell of canned dog food. To make sure that the dog, Pulgoso, would look at me when I talked to him, his trainer would stand behind me with dog food on her hands so that he would smell it and look at her. She would hold five fingers over my head, dripping greasy morsels of food onto my scalp and leaving me with the unbearable stench of a butcher.

Also during *Marimar,* I remember a scene in which the character of Angélica, the hero's stepmother, threw a bracelet in the mud and made me take it out with my mouth. My director, Beatriz Sheridan, took great care of me so that I would not contract any type of sickness from swallowing actual mud that might contain bacteria or other contaminants, and with the set design team she decided to build a little simulated puddle of mud using chocolate. They placed a piece of plastic beneath it and melted one hundred bars of chocolate, but it didn't work; from the beginning it had an odd texture. After we shot the scene of me bobbing for the bracelet with my mouth in the mud-chocolate, when we looked at the playback, there was an unnatural-looking orange color around my mouth. It definitely looked like a puddle of fake mud, so I said, "Betty, I don't have a problem with this scene; let's do it the right way," even though I didn't want to! But the lousy shot we had and my insistence led us to shoot the scene in a realistic, natural environment. We filmed the scene exactly as it was, and that was how it stayed. I had to do it. It was the scene that would determine the vengeance of Marimar; it was the climax of the story and it needed to be as realistic as possible. People still tell me they cry when they watch it, because the shame on Marimar's face was so intense.

In *María la del Barrio* I also lived through many intense moments that were loaded with adrenaline. María made a living gathering bottles from trash dumps, and we filmed at an actual garbage dump in Mexico City. It smelled like cadavers and dead rats all the time. And we spent hours there! I could not cover my face because of my character, but I also didn't do it because, instead of resting during breaks, I would use the time to chat with the scavengers who make a living digging through garbage, just like María la del Barrio. While they scavenged through the mountains of real trash, I dug around in my own little "fake" trash built by the prop team, so that I, or anyone on the crew, would never be risking our health. Seeing kids rummaging through garbage to find something to eat, or to search for little cars, dolls or any other toys that they would make their own, marked me for life. Months later, I would come back with food and toys for these families who lived at the edges of the trash dump.

It was always important for me to talk to the real people, the ones who had inspired the writers to create my characters; to speak with the María Mercedeses, with the Miramars, and with the Marías *del barrio*. When we stopped shooting, between takes, I would approach the scavengers and say, "Hi, what's up? Why is your baby in diapers running around all over the garbage? Aren't you worried that he will get sick?" And they would respond, "No, sweetie, they are used to it." That affected me so much! This was the kind of place where you could find everything from animal skulls to human hands and feet, and fetuses in varying degrees of decomposition. It was really intense! When I walked amid the garbage, the earth moved beneath me like a living carpet; it was the rats and cockroaches scurrying under plastic bags, boxes, papers or cartons. It was like an ever-shifting rug. The moment we would wrap, I would run directly to my dressing room to take a shower. I don't know if it was because I wanted to get rid of that stench, or because I needed to scrub away those horrendous images that swirled around in my mind.

Those are the moments, although strong and crude in some cases, that I still treasure as extraordinary experiences in my career as an actress.

Other moments that would wear me out and frustrate me were the ones in which I had to really cry, immersed in my character, actually feeling the pain and sheer suffering, when all of a sudden . . . "*Cut!* A light moved." *What? Who said that?* I wanted to kill the guy who yelled it out and the guy who didn't steady the light, because in acting, being able to recover that moment is very, very hard. You can do it if you are a good soap opera actor, so that you can get through as many takes as needed. But in that first moment, your whole essence is overwhelmed, and the atoms of your cells don't seem to come back to you. To reshoot, to capture that initial sentiment, is never easy.

In *Rosalinda* we did a similar scene to the one with the cliff in *Marimar*. Rosalinda goes crazy and is on the brink of jumping from the top of a building, a scene once again filmed without the use of a safety net below, without a harness, with nothing, not even a mattress to land on. There was a moment when I thought, *If I wanted to jump right now, I would certainly die on the way.* I didn't have suicidal thoughts or anything like that, but I realized that I was taking too great a risk without needing to. I was always at the edge of danger—something that I would never do today.

My Own Rhythm

In my music career, the path has been intense and very productive, like everything. Along with my songs I continued to transform, renew and reinvent. I began my recording career on vinyl records of thirty-three revolutions, or forty-fives when they were singles. I continued with cassettes or tapes, to later move on to CDs, and now I am in the era of streaming and clouds. Moving forward with technology, I cannot imagine what would have happened if social networks had been a part of my professional life from the very beginning. To think that without the marvelous tool that is the Internet, which in seconds sends my name to the other side of the world, along with information about my career, I still managed to become successful in more than 180 countries in the world, with the only tools that I had in reach: television, radio and the written word. I often ask myself, How would my career have developed if the Internet had existed at its beginning? For these new generations, fame is instantaneous, and whether you sing, dance or simply make an entertaining YouTube video so that millions of people will recognize your name, today anyone can become famous instantly. It's a great advantage, but it does give new artists a lot of competition.

But as appealing as the thought of instant fame may be, I prefer the path when you reap what you actually sow, where experiences transform into lessons, and where fame doesn't result from the click of a video, but instead an arsenal of experience and firm steps that become the pillars of support that hold us up during the years to come. I wouldn't change those experiences for anything in the world, because they made me who I am today; they are what define me as a person, as an artist and as a woman. And for that I am eternally grateful.

With many multiplatinum albums recorded and seven soap

operas in the can, the best thing I ever received, the greatest honor that was ever given to me, has been the satisfaction of being accepted by my audience, an audience that transcends borders, races and languages. To know that my characters reached and continue to reach the homes of millions of people, accompanying them each day and making them dream a little through these stories, is for me overwhelming in the best way possible. It moves me deeply. When I remember the eighteen-year-old girl who hid in bed for two whole weeks because of the criticism and lack of acceptance from her audience, and now see her triumphant and, along with her three Marías, loved and accepted by people of so many races, languages and cultures—this reward does not compare to anything!

· CHAPTER THREE ·

FREEDOM

D*ear Freedom:*

Precious and unmatched friend, how long did I live without properly knowing you? How many days, how many nights and how many hours did I exist walking in the arms of captivity, which over time made every possible effort so that you and I would never find each other? At some point, captivity managed to keep me locked in the darkness of every negative thought that it would place inside my heart; it tried to immobilize me, locking me up in chains of anxiety, pain and solitude; it insisted on taking me by the hand, guiding me straight to the traps it had purposefully set along my path; but it was not able to deter our meeting that had been scheduled for all of eternity.

Our time came, and when I least expected it, we were face-to-face. Your sense of love and patience are so great, my beloved Freedom, that with such tenderness and care, you managed to remove the locks and chains that I had been dragging around all along the way.

You embraced me, you wrapped me up and I could at last breathe so deeply that I could finally be conscious of myself, my space, my being, my very essence.

Freedom, your name is so lovely; it contains Eternity.

By your side, I was able to free myself from one of the greatest battles.

I was able to overcome and prevail triumphantly against the captivity of my mind . . . toward freedom.

Freedom

The frenetic pace at which I was working was beginning to become unmanageable. I felt exhausted all the time, ragged, without energy or strength. I still loved my career and the people with whom I worked, the trips, and the privilege of being able to perform onstage in front of an audience who knew my songs. But I had arrived at a point where I had to—*needed* to—stop. I knew in the deepest part of my soul that I needed a change; I needed freedom, and my first ally on this search was the moon, which one night became my friend.

I was on a musical tour through South America, and one of the shows was held outdoors. The warm and tropical climate made the moment uniquely special for me, as the breeze caressed me and played with my hair. . . . I lifted my gaze, and all of a sudden, like an apparition seen in the middle of the night, I saw the biggest, most magnificent moon that I had ever beheld; it was right in front of me, and I watched it intently as I sang. Suddenly, when I got to the bridge of one of the songs, I started talking directly to the moon, my words ascending into the sky, and with all my heart, I began to say, "My eyes are seeing this moon, and I know that the eyes of the man who will be the love of my life, someone I have not yet met, are also seeing it. . . ." Just then, I felt my whole being vibrate from top to bottom with such intensity that the moment seemed to last forever. "I know you are out there," I went on. "I know that you are also feeling me right now, and that we will soon meet . . . soon we will love each other. I don't know where you are, or where you live . . . I don't know who you are, but tonight I'm feeling you . . . during this very precious moment." My feelings were so intense that the tears streamed down my face. "I know that love is real," I told myself, "and I know that you exist and that you are there for me."

And it was then that I clearly felt that this person, this man, would be waiting for me with the same excitement and sense of certainty, ready for the day destiny would unite us forever.

The Rebel

I was able to confirm the certainty that my true love was waiting for me somewhere in the universe one day at my sister Titi's house, with a friend of hers who was a psychic. Back then, I carried a great pain in my heart; my first love—the Rebel—had recently passed away. Ours had been love at first sight: We were leaving a gathering with friends and, at a certain point, he and I found ourselves face-to-face. There was no escaping it; our gazes were destined to meet. It was one of those looks that affirm the sense that you have encountered this soul in a different body, or in another space and time. You know that your spirits have already been together, that they intuit each other. The glance we exchanged on that day was so intense and powerful that we both imagined what could happen—it immediately shook us and forcefully separated us, because we knew that we could not control what was coming.

And even so, it came. From the instant we met, I felt wildly attracted to him, both physically and intellectually. I loved that he was a free spirit, a man who was never afraid to break rules, say no, and go beyond what was expected of him. He was a rebel in every sense of the word, and his energy inspired and moved me in such a powerful way. Having spent practically my entire life in show business, a business that required me to say yes all the time, I was intoxicated and refreshed by his perspective. I became so enamored with him that soon we were spending all our time together.

We had everything and nothing in common, and it was one of those relationships that consumes your whole being, and even though we wanted to stay apart, we felt like we were meant for each other. Our relationship lasted for several years, and the time we spent together was very passionate, fun, intimate, and intense—all of which fused us into one being. We were inseparable, and the physical attraction we felt for each other was totally beyond our control. But at the same time, our relationship contained a self-destructive element—the power with which we adored each other was so intense, lustful and so devastatingly obsessive that we had a very difficult time spending time apart from each other. It was like the moth that sees the flame of a candle and, despite getting burned, continues to remain transfixed by the light, sacrificing itself for the beauty of the light. That's how our days passed, tumultuously battling against this uncontrollable love, and knowing deep down in our hearts that despite our desire to build a life together, it was never going to happen.

Even so, with the illusion of love in his soul, one day my Rebel showed up with an engagement ring in his hand and asked me to marry him. Oblivious of the many problems we had—perhaps we thought that by getting married they would all fade away—we began to make plans for our wedding. We were both excited about the prospect of sharing our lives forever. But as much as we tried to ignore the bad in order to focus on the good, the problems that had plagued our relationship for so many years quickly reemerged. Especially his jealousy. My Rebel was always a jealous man, but after our engagement our lives became a living hell. He became jealous of my on-screen kisses, jealous of my dancers when they would touch me, jealous of my wardrobe people. . . . It was like there was nothing I could do without him getting upset at me. It wasn't that our relationship was abusive, it was just an unhealthy obsession. We fought all the time.

One night we were out dancing at a club in Acapulco when I ran into an old friend of mine whom I was very happy to see. I stepped off the dance floor for a moment to talk to him and catch up, but when the Rebel saw me talking to another man, he simply lost it. Right then and there he started yelling at me, and at one point he even grabbed my hand and pulled me away over to a corner, where he continued to yell a thousand insults. When I think back on it, I can't even remember what he was saying; the only thing that remained forever etched in my mind was the distant and furious look in his eyes; he seemed possessed. At that moment I realized that our relationship had reached a new low and there was nothing we could do to trust each other again.

So we broke up. Our connection, however, was so deep that we continued to attract each other like a couple of magnets. Even though in my soul I wanted nothing other than to be with him for the rest of my life, in my mind I knew it was simply impossible. Neither he nor I could continue such an exhausting situation. We put a final end to the relationship, and in order not to think too much about it, I dived right in to my newest project, which at the time was *Marimar*.

Time went by, and although we were able to get used to being apart, both our hearts were aching. We stopped seeing each other but we still spoke on the phone. At the time several of my friends told me it was his love for me that was killing him; he was completely distraught. And while I had plunged into my work and was managing to stay busy in order to forget the pain I was experiencing, the Rebel returned to his extreme and destructive behaviors. I knew that he was not doing well with his health; the doctors had told him he had to stop his excessive ways before it was too late. But, of course, being the rebel that he was, he never listened.

One day while I was shooting on location, while the whole crew sat together for a meal in the gardens of the Hacienda Santibañez, my mother received a phone call. With the cell phone in her hand, her whole face changed, and I knew right away that the news was not good. My mother lowered the phone, grabbed me by the arm and took me away from the table, embraced me with great compassion and said, "Daughter, they just informed me . . . he just died."

I grabbed the phone away from her hand and asked the person on the other end of the line, "Who? Who just died?"

The voice on the other end confirmed what I had already somehow suspected inside my heart. . . . My Rebel had passed away. I set off running aimlessly, my legs moving toward a field, as far away from where I had been as I could get. I cried and shook, and at one point I stopped to rest under a tree, as I felt that my heart was going to burst. My pain was indescribable; I screamed from the deepest part of my being—I just couldn't comprehend the fact that my soul mate was never going to be with me again. My father's death intensely came to my mind. I thought of how my father had died as a result of my love kiss, and now my Rebel had died because of my love kiss. Both men had known they were sick, but both had chosen to let themselves die. "Why did you abandon me?" I screamed to him, as if he could hear me. "Why did you leave? Why did you leave me?" Right at that moment a breeze came by, agitating everything, especially the white flowers that bloomed from the tree under which I sat. A light rain of white flowers drizzled onto me, like a soft, healing balm, consoling me and almost saying, "Here I am, and I will always be here . . . always by your side." And from that moment on, his presence was close to me on countless occasions, until that day in my sister Titi's house.

That day, my sister had invited a group of her friends under the pretext that a very talented psychic was going to attend, and since I had nothing else to do and nothing to lose, I decided to join them. Some of the guests had their fortunes told, while others pounced upon the food in my sister's kitchen. Finally, it was my turn. We sat in a private area of the house and the psychic began to tell me about my future, but just then the woman's attitude became agitated and she said, "You know, there is someone present in the room with us right now." I instantly felt the hairs stand up on the back of my neck. How could someone be in the room with us? A ghost, a soul, a spirit? *How scary*, I thought. The woman went on to describe my Rebel to a T, and I said to myself skeptically, *She probably researched my whole life just to delude me.* And it was then that she went on to describe things that only he and I knew, intimate moments that we had lived that no one, not even my sisters, could have found out. She said, "He is here because he wants you to know that he has already seen the man who is going to take care of you. He wants to tell you not to be afraid of giving yourself to love, that you should not run away from this one, because he is a man who is going to adore you and care for you with total honesty and a sincere love."

"That is why I am here," said my Rebel, "to inform you that I am leaving your life. Until now, I have taken care of you, but soon the one who is going to take care of you from now on will arrive, and everything will be fine." In that moment, I experienced a catharsis. It was a blend of sorrow, love, joy, surprise and, oddly, liberation. He would leave, I would rest, and at the same time I would be free of the blame that I felt for my father's death, and for my Rebel's. I left that room feeling revitalized, changed and liberated . . . open to love.

And that is how my search began.

As I waited for the question that I had launched into the universe to come back with an answer for me, my career continued to progress in huge leaps, a crazy frenzy, a hurricane in which every time I would lift my gaze I would find no escape and see no light; I felt an internal void, an insatiable hole in my soul.

Anxiety and Phobias

Naturally, I lived through situations that were beyond my control; just as my career became more solid, it also became a lot more complex. I wanted everything to be perfect, for things to always play out just as I had planned them. Today I understand that this is impossible when you work as part of a team, that it is not just you alone, but rather many people who are involved in a particular project, and any of these individuals can make a mistake. Or I might face unpredictable situations, such as when my costume would tear right before a scene, or when we would be late to a show, or when one of my musicians wouldn't show up . . . or when, for example, five minutes before starting the show, the zipper of my dress got stuck and broke—what adrenaline! Of course, my costume designer would come prepared with a special little fanny pack loaded with everything necessary: needles already prepared with different-colored threads, pins of all sizes, Band-Aids, tape, headache medicine and anything else that could solve an immediate problem. . . . There were moments in which my wardrobe person had to hurriedly sew the dress right on my body, as there was no time to take it off. So that was how I went out; I would sing the song and upon my return tear open the dress to put on the next one. Backstage it was total madness.

The truth is that any one of those situations could make me feel bad to the point that it would make my mind start to race, like a hamster treading upon its little wheel, running and running in circles without stopping until wearing out, without moving from its place; that's how my mind was—it dominated me in such a way that I often didn't sleep. I needed to control my mind, I needed to shed my skin and I needed to free myself.

Sometimes we had work meetings to plan our strategy for moving forward. Whenever things did not play out the way that I had organized them in my head, my "hamster" would start to run, spinning and spinning its little wheel, with my thoughts bombarding me and constantly repeating, *Why didn't I tell them to do it like this? Why did I stay quiet and not respond? How could I let them talk to me this way?* And I would repeat these questions over and over again, playing the imaginary scene inside my mind, and basically talking to myself, saying everything that I had not said in the moment. What torture, what a total prison; and the result was that I was never satisfied with what I had done, and even when my crew would say, "You're so amazing. . . . You were phenomenal to-night!" I would never believe it.

It took me many years to understand everything that took place, with the help of experienced psychologists and my own research in books about psychology, self-esteem and spirituality. In time, I learned how to stop along my own path; I learned to see myself, to be conscious of my thoughts, and to stop the crazy frenzy that would sometimes unhinge me. Although I have to admit there were times when the "hamster" returned to treading upon its little wheel, around and around, until the moment that I would become aware of this whirlwind of ideas and consciously stop "the wheel."

Among so many different types of therapies, I learned about the importance of finding tools that could work for me, be it via breathing, reading or meditation. One of the exercises that would calm me down and bring me back to the present involved the use of my mantra. It is necessary to have a strategic word that you say out loud when you find yourself caught in a vicious cycle of neg-ative thinking—something like, "I heard you, thank you," some-thing that allows you to return to the present, and stops you from living inside a thought pattern that doesn't reflect reality.

Another thing that saved me and gave back my calm was to seek outdoor activities, such as rock climbing, yoga and hiking. These activities helped me discover a real sense of balance for my body, mind and soul, and to this very day I give them priority above any other commitment that I may have. My battle unfolded directly against myself, and was made difficult because of the phobias that developed throughout the course of my life, and as a result of the thoughts that had become repetitive. But gradually I came back, I forced myself to return to my present, and I took on the obligation to take care of myself.

From the age of eighteen, I began to desire, to yearn for and need my independence; my life had become exclusively focused on my career, and I didn't have the opportunity or desire to think about anything else. My mother, whose love I never, ever doubted, for the first time in her life was able to develop her own career as a manager that was parallel to mine; so the combination of my mother-manager, manager-mother fused to such a degree that for a long time it was impossible to separate them; her way of working on me, for me and with me practically turned me into a disabled person. She always had everything organized; everything was already done, solved; there was nothing ever to learn, nothing to know, and all I knew was how to devote myself to me.

So, like any young person at that age, I began to feel the need to experiment with the prospect of living alone. Even though my mother had never been too possessive or domineering with me, or at least she never let me see it, I longed to embark on my own personal adventure. Knowing that through my work I could easily support myself and be financially independent gave me the feeling that I didn't need people telling me what to do, or when to do it.

While I lived in Mexico, my mother and I had a beautiful house that was designed by the architect Miguel Aragones, one of the most renowned young architects of the day. He had built it in an exclusive area of Mexico City. The house was way too big, so my mother lived on one floor, and I lived on another. This gave me enough freedom to come and go as I pleased at whatever hour I wanted, without having to give too many explanations. So it was "each man for himself"; in other words, we both had our own separate lives. I would go out dancing with my friends until dawn; then we would end up eating the classic *taquitos al pastor,* with their little slices of pineapple and a few drops of lemon, and a very spicy sauce for that hour of the morning . . . and the little tacos would gradually vanish one by one, leaving the plate clean. After that, everyone would go home, where they would sleep a couple of hours. However, there were days when I would get to my house with just enough time to take a shower, throw on a pair of pants and go running to Televisa to make an early call time. I would arrive like a zombie and sit on a chair for my hair and makeup, and then wardrobe. I honestly didn't complain, because somehow or other I was able to go out and enjoy myself a bit, amid so much hard and demanding work; I went out to laugh and dance with my friends, which were really just a few—but to me they were a potent multitude.

From the age of nineteen to twenty, I went about my work rhythm in forced strides. Soap opera after soap opera, *palenque* after *palenque,* show after show, so my escapes were very important; they were the quickest way for me to release the pressure that I held within.

Every soap opera came with its own set of challenges, and each one demanded more and more from me. But during *María la del Barrio,* I had an actual nervous breakdown. The last few episodes were to be done live, and I felt that the entire weight of the soap opera rested on me. If there was ever a moment when I longed to return to theater, well, at the end of the soap opera I practically did, because just like in the theater, we couldn't say, "Do it over." The images went directly via satellite to the homes of hundreds of thousands of people—without any previous rehearsals. The only take was the one that came out, and that would have to be the best take. There was no way to redo it and no other options. My anxiety was so intense during those days of shooting that we ended up having an emergency meeting in Salvador Mejía's office, together with Valentin Pimstein and Emilio Azcárraga Milmo. I was shaking with anxiety, and I kept repeating, "I can't do this anymore. . . . I just can't do it anymore." Emilio, apart from being one of the high-ranking executives of the company at the time (today he's the chairman of Televisa), had also become a very close friend; he hugged me and said, "Don't worry; everything is going to be okay. We will see what we can do."

I was trapped inside my own exhaustion, inside the pressure of everything that was going on, inside my own desperation, so I took Emilio's hand and squeezed it so strongly that I caught his attention and conveyed my real emotional state: "Emilio, don't you understand that I just want a regular life? I want to be a normal woman! I want to be just like everyone else; I want peace and tranquillity. . . . I just can't take this responsibility anymore. . . . I can't do it! It's just too much pressure for me. . . . I dream of being a mother, of having a family; when is that going to happen? Do you understand what I am saying? If I don't get back on the stage soon, the show will not air tonight. Do you understand what I am saying?"

They gave me some tranquilizers and I went back to my dressing room while they deliberated over what to do. They concluded that I needed to rest for a while, so they gave me two weeks off and decided to send me to my house in Los Angeles, and they would somehow figure it out. And they sorted it out well by airing reruns of *María la del Barrio*'s best episodes, while I attempted to recover.

Of course, it was a nervous breakdown because of everything that had happened. But this was just the tip of the iceberg, because deep down I wanted to totally free myself from the world of soap operas, along with the weight of the chains that held me down.

But still, not everything was so dramatic or complicated. In the midst of how difficult my work could be at times, I never lost my essential sense of fun-loving mischief. I dated a lot, partied and had a great time, and thank God I never got into drugs; just thinking about it would make me nervous, because the pattern of behavior in my family was addictive and compulsive, and I knew that if I ever tried a drug, there would be no end to it. And there was no shortage of opportunities, since I had been a television star and singer from a young age, so everything came my way— pills, cocaine, marijuana—all of which people generously wanted to give me as gifts, but knowing my family history, I would run from them, always viewing them from a distance, with fear. But on the other hand, my "tequilitas," vodkas and margaritas . . . went down like water! I did gladly partake of those, and I would enjoy myself to the end. The laughter, the jokes and dancing were my great escape, a way for me to rebel against my mother, who wouldn't stop telling me whom to date or not. But I would play dumb and date whomever I wanted.

When we were home, I had a certain level of autonomy and my own life that was outside my mother's circle. But when we traveled, we were together every minute. And besides being her daughter, I was an artist whom she managed, which oftentimes caused us to clash. Apart from this type of hectic life, certain events that I endured started to provoke a series of phobias in me that would accompany me for a good portion of my life, making me a slave to them day after day.

These habits would manifest themselves at the most unexpected moments, and caused in me a sense of tension that was extremely difficult to control. One of the events that detonated those phobias happened when I was sixteen years old, and my sister Federica and I went to eat burgers at a new place that had just opened up near my old high school. The place was full of students, mostly junior and high school students, which was why, when we arrived, we went all the way to the back of the restaurant, close to a large window, so that we could watch the people strolling by on the street, while we sat to eat our burgers. At the time I had just started out in Timbiriche, and when they saw me, many of the students who were there came over to me to ask for my autograph. I signed some of them, but there were so many that I said, "Guys, my burger is going to get cold; let me finish eating and we'll continue later." I never imagined what was going to happen: Around thirty or so young boys approached our table, hurling insults at me for not signing autographs for them at that exact moment. They started to pound on the table with their fists, and the expressions on their faces turned mocking and threatening. . . . It was the kind of thing that happens only in groups, what one would consider as bullying. I got very nervous, but I was able to control myself. Thank God Federica reacted fast; she stood up and got me out of there. As we walked toward the exit, the boys made way, but not without a good amount of jostling, their hands threatening us with each bump. We got out to the street and into the car, and the instant the car door closed, I broke down in tears. . . . All I wanted was to eat a burger!

This was one of the first phobias that I acquired: the fear of having too many people around me, closing in on my space. On many occasions I was forced to face this social phobia. Another incident that reinforced the episode with the hamburgers occurred when we were performing a show and the Timbiriche fans all wanted a photograph or an autograph from us. There was a great crowd of young people who saw us get in our van and surrounded the vehicle. We had all the windows closed and they wanted us to open them so that they could pass through their photographs, albums, T-shirts and anything else that we could sign. When we didn't, the boys started to shake the car from one side to the other, and for a moment I thought the van would actually flip over. Panic struck right away, and I don't even know how we got out of there; and even though nothing happened in the end, that moment of vulnerability has always stayed with me.

These types of experiences started to create a tremendous amount of physical and emotional apprehension in me. I started to develop certain types of habits. To be honest, I became as compulsive as the Jack Nicholson character in *As Good As It Gets,* who would turn the lights on and off repeatedly, and engage and disengage the lock on his door multiple times before setting foot outside of his apartment; or Leonardo DiCaprio's character in *The Aviator,* who would wash his hands compulsively until they bled. In the spirit of jest, my family even referred to me as Howard Hughes well before that film was ever released.

Many years passed before I understood what made me behave so obsessively. The doctor with whom I worked to recover from my phobias made me understand that sometimes there are just too many changes in our lives; they feel like air that cannot be captured, or like water, which you can hold but eventually it slowly drips through your fingers. When there is no sense of structure to the life you lead, you can subconsciously start to develop what is known as agoraphobia, an anxiety disorder that consists of the fear of being out somewhere and having a panic attack with nowhere to get help; in essence, it can be defined as the fear of fear. Among the fears felt by agoraphobics are the loss of control or looking foolish to the point of being afraid to leave one's home. So, as I developed my obsessions and habits, these little rituals that I had created, what I was really looking for was a sense of security, to feel that I had control over my life and mind.

I know perfectly well that we really cannot control anything, but it's one thing to know something and another thing to truly understand it. Every day I still must overcome these types of thoughts, the ones that awaken the phobias in me; when I feel vulnerable, I take a deep breath, I think of something beautiful—like a sun-kissed beach and me sitting underneath a palm tree, calm, feeling the breeze of the ocean against my skin—and continuing to breathe deeply, I arrive at tranquillity and gain control of myself.

While I struggled to gain my personal equilibrium, my workload became even heavier, making me want to leave it all behind. I kept telling myself over and over again that I had the right to create a life of my own . . . but my thoughts were ambivalent and caused me tremendous distress. I thought, *How can I leave my mother alone when she dedicated herself entirely to me?* Besides, I didn't think my mother was ready to leave me.

Still, in the midst of all this stress due to my professional and personal life, I met the love of my life, an Italian New Yorker who would spin my existence in an entirely different direction. I never could have imagined how things were going to play out, but just a few months after I met him, I decided to launch myself on an adventure, and moved from Mexico to New York City.

A Cupid Named Emilio

It all started in 1992, when I was invited to participate in one of the most important music festivals, national or international, which was slated to take place in Acapulco. It was organized and directed by Raúl Velasco, one of the most prominent television hosts of the day. In fact, every musical artist of the time wanted an invitation to appear on Raúl Velasco's television show, *Siempre en*

Domingo (*Always on Sunday*), because anyone he featured was guaranteed to have success. Many renowned figures came to Mexico to take part in the festival, including Rocío Dúrcal, Rafael, and Julio Iglesias, along with Italian, American and Brazilian artists, among many others. It was here that I had the great fortune of meeting Emilio Estefan, husband of the ever-famous Gloria Estefan.

We were staying at a villa at the Las Brisas hotel, which is very famous in Acapulco. I was in a bathing suit, enjoying the sun, when all of a sudden, my mother started screaming down from our balcony.

"*Flaca! Flaca!* . . . Here!" she said as she waved her arm to get someone's attention. "Thalita and I are up here. . . . What are you up to?"

And "*Flaca,*" who was none other than Lili Estefan—niece of Gloria and Emilio Estefan—responded to her greeting by inviting us to her villa.

"Yolanda, why don't you come over here? My uncle is here, so you can meet him. . . ."

A few months before we had been in Miami on the radio show produced by Lili Estefan, and my mother, daring as she is, had asked if we might meet her uncle, because she wanted him to record one of my albums. Lili very generously promised that it would happen as soon as the opportunity came up. But the chance came without our having to wait for it. And Yolanda Miranda, known in the industry as "El Doctor Cerebro" ("Dr. Brain"), was not going to let that moment pass for anything in the world. She screamed, "Thalita! Come over here; what are you doing sitting over there? Come on over because we have to go meet him. Throw on a wrap or sarong over your bathing suit and let's go, come on!"

And that is just what we did. We jumped in a little golf cart, which was the only way to travel from one villa to another, and when we arrived at Lili's, we saw "El Gordo de Molina," who at the time was a paparazzo, and who was taking photographs of Jon Secada, Lili and Emilio Estefan. Without further ado, my mother introduced herself to them: "Hi, I'm Yolanda Miranda, and this is Thalia."

She enthusiastically said hello to Lili and Emilio; when I came over to say hello, Emilio looked at me and said, "Of course I know who you are. You entertain us at home. Do you know that Glorita is a huge fan of *Marimar*, and she has her mother and me sit and watch it with her every afternoon?"

They watch my soap opera? I thought. *And they don't miss an episode!* I was deeply affected, and never would have imagined that they watched me every day in the living room of their home. I ended up, together with Jon Secada and Lili, in the pool for the photo shoot. Of course, while all of this was going on, my mother was already talking to Emilio, practically finalizing the agreement to record an album with him.

"Emilio," my mother said very seriously, "you are the King Midas of the music world, and my daughter is the Queen Midas of television ratings. You have to join forces and record an album. She is already working on one now, but at least give her one song."

At the time I was in the middle of recording what was going to be my fourth album, *En Éxtasis* (*In Ecstasy*), leaving Fonovisa to join EMI Latin, while simultaneously promoting my third album, *Love*, with songs like *"Sangre,"* which I wrote, *"La Vida en Rosa,"* a Spanish adaptation of the famous Edith Piaf song *"La Vie en Rose,"* *"Maria Mercedes,"* and the title track, "Love." "Sangre" and "Love" became hits, and, in fact, I had been doing really well. My last few albums had already gone gold and platinum many times over and I was ready for more. If the next one was going to be with

Emilio Estefan, it would be completely Glorious (pun intended) for me. . . .

Emilio, ever the gentleman, kept telling my insistent mother, "Yes, woman, but let's take some time to think about it," trying to defer the conversation to another time.

"Come on, Thalita . . . sing for him, so he can hear what you sound like. . . ." And, of course, I wanted to disappear.

What did she mean, "sing for him, so he can hear what you sound like"? Did she not see that everyone was lounging around the pool? It was clearly neither the time nor the place. Emilio took note of the stormy moment, and asked my mother when we were planning to come to Miami.

"Tomorrow, if need be," she answered immediately, and he told her to call him when we were there, that he would be waiting in his studio. But he said he was sorry, that though he would love for us to come by, he could not guarantee anything, because he didn't really want to be anyone's producer, other than his wife's or Jon Secada's, both of whose careers he dedicated himself to managing.

Months later, Cristina Saralegui invited me onto her show. When we got back to my hotel after filming *El Show de Cristina*, there was a message for me from Crescent Moon Studios—Emilio's office—telling me to come over. My mother and I again jumped up and down on the bed like two crazies. If everything went well, this appointment could mark the crossover of my musical career.

Just like that, we arrived at Crescent Moon Studios. Emilio Estefan is one of the world's leading musical impresarios, with great vision for music, business and the selection of his artists, and since we'd met in Acapulco he had been following my career. He was already familiar with my music. My mother and I, who were ridiculously nervous but totally euphoric, walked into that grand office that was decorated with gold and platinum records and magazine covers featuring an array of Gloria's work.

As we looked at all the awards and recognitions, Emilio walked in and greeted us.

"I have a song that I want you to sing. It was for Gloria, but I don't know why the song screams 'Thalia' every time I hear the lyrics." He flashed me that ample smile, and on his sound system, which took up an entire wall from floor to ceiling, with speakers of every size and the most sophisticated sound equipment that I had ever seen, he played the first chords of the song. I could feel all the hairs on my body stand up, from my feet to my head . . . It was *"Piel Morena"* ("Brown Skin").

After hearing the song, I said, "Can I record it? I will go into the studio and record it right away." I looked straight into his eyes.

Emilio laughed.

"Don't worry; we have a lot of time ahead of us for you to learn the song and rehearse it." He didn't think that I was capable of recording just like that, without rehearsing. I came from the school of Marta Zabaleta and Julissa during the *Vaselina* era, and I was trained by Luis de Llano for Timbiriche, where everything was "learn it in five minutes and we'll record it." With the pace of soap operas, where the script changed from one moment to the next and the scenes had to be rehearsed and filmed in one day, my brain had turned into a sponge. It was trained to absorb dialogue, songs and choreography, and it was capable of memorizing in seconds and executing right away.

I said to myself, *This song is done; I'll go into the studio now and we'll have it in three takes . . . period. We'll print it.* I insisted so much that even though Emilio was not convinced, he called the composer, Kike Santander, to come over; he wanted to see just how far the "Mexicanita" could go. Half an hour later the man whom we were waiting for arrived. I reviewed the song two or three times, he corrected a few of my notes, and there, before everyone's stunned eyes, *"Piel Morena"* was born, and became one of my most successful worldwide hits.

Love Arrives

At the same time I finished shooting *María la del Barrio,* I also ended my relationship with Fernando Colunga, something that came about from the soap operas. I pass this fact along to all his fans: Fernando is a gentleman in every sense of the word—sweet, tender, fun and a wonderful friend.

Since I was going to Miami a lot to see Emilio and work on my next album, Emilio and I developed a very sincere friendship. There were moments in which he served as a shoulder to cry on, as, apart from being my producer, he had become one of my closest friends. He and Gloria have a solid wonderful marriage, something that I had always aspired to. So I told him about my relationships and about all my failed attempts to find the man of my dreams, my knight in shining armor. Our work relationship had transformed into a close feeling of family, and when my mother and I would arrive in Florida, the Estefans would always be waiting for us with lunch or dinner.

During one of those conversations in which I told him about my love life, he said, "My little one . . . you are a queen and I know the perfect person for you. . . . I am sure he is your king."

I looked at him pointedly, as if to say, *Don't you even think about it; I don't want to meet anyone.* Still, Emilio did not give up, and kept telling me about this king of his, Tommy Mottola, who was also his friend and going through something similar. I had no idea who this person was; nor was I interested in finding out, to be honest. But Emilio never missed a chance to bring him up. "One of these days the two of you have to meet, go out for a drink, at least. You are so much alike, like two drops of water!" he would say over and over again.

One day I inquired a bit more about this character, and Emilio gave me more details. He told me that he had been married twice, that he had two children, that he was older than me, and that he lived in New York. My eyes widened so much that Emilio looked troubled. What kind of guy did he want to set me up with? Me, coming out of all my travails, and he wanted to set me up with this load of complications?! But like the Mexican proverb says, "Weddings and funerals are determined only by the heavens." So a whole year after Emilio brought up the topic of Mottola, we had our first date.

I flew to New York because I had been invited to participate in an independent film. My mother and agents thought it would be a huge waste of time and didn't want me to do it, because they felt that it didn't make sense, after doing internationally famous soap operas, to go to the United States for something small and low-budget. But I needed a change of scenery. I wanted to try something different and leave my routine and the television studios. Just like that, I packed up and went to New York for a few months. I had just spent a month traveling to various music festivals in Spain and France, promoting my fifth album *Amor a la Mexicana* (*Love the Mexican Way*) in all its versions and remixes; I was pleased to find out that the hit "*Amor a la Mexicana*" became the summer anthem of Europe. Since I already had with me the script for the film, while I traveled through the continent I rehearsed as often as I could, and memorized it phonetically (my English was barely a two on a scale from one to ten!). The producers had recorded all the dialogue and sent me the cassettes, so that I could learn the lines just as I heard them, by memory.

When I finished my tour, I flew right back to my house in Los Angeles; I needed a few more weeks to refine the accent and pronunciation. And from there, I went directly to New York, where I spent three months shooting the film. The last day of filming, I called Emilio and said, "Tomorrow is my day off. I am going shopping, to the theater, and then I am going back to Mexico. Listen, Emilio, why don't you tell that friend of yours you're always talking about to call me so we can go out? One drink, okay? No dinners or anything like that. Because blowing a whole meal and putting up with a guy who is just going to annoy me, well, you know that's not for me." His euphoria could be felt all the way on the other end of the line, as he was finally going to get his way. He didn't waste a second, and called his friend right away.

Later, Tommy told me that when Emilio called him, he said, "Tommy, remember my friend whom I wanted to introduce you to? A queen for a king, my friend. She's in Manhattan; call her to go out; she is waiting for your call."

"Listen, Emilio," Tommy said right away, "it really isn't the best time for me to go out with anyone. . . . I'll take her out for one drink, okay? No dinner or anything like that."

He, too, didn't want anything serious with anyone.

It was very cold and snowing, so I arrived at the place all bundled up in my coat. When I walked into the restaurant, the host led me to the bar, which was located down a flight of stairs. The place was very Italian, with candles on the tables, which made it very romantic. I wore an ivory coat and my hair long and loose, very much like Marimar. Of all the men who were there, a very handsome one stood out, holding a chilled martini in his hand, and as I walked down the stairs, I prayed that it was he, because from the moment I saw him I felt an enormous attraction. The host did seem to be leading us toward the handsome man, and it was then that he smiled at me and I knew that he was Tommy Mottola. Now that I think about it, God knows I would have simply left if I hadn't liked him. Luckily, that's not what happened!

That night we talked for hours, and I honestly don't know what we could have talked about, since my English was not very good, and I could just barely get by with the basics. Still, he managed to understand everything that I said; but what really mitigated my precarious English was memorizing the script from the film that I had just finished shooting! Based on my interpretation of his body language, I would shoot off some English phrase from the script, and it seemed to work very well, because he even laughed—leaving me no doubt that this independent film had a reason for being.

I loved everything about Tommy from the first moment; he was so gallant, so manly, so mature. . . . I didn't remember ever meeting a man of this caliber. Sitting at that table and barely knowing him, I was already filled with a sense of security and tranquillity, and I felt that I could say anything to him and he would be able to handle it. From the first instant, I realized that he was a man with an open mind, and to this day it is one of the things about him that I like the most.

When we said good-bye to each other, he respectfully asked for a second date. He said, "So, when do I see you again?" And I answered him with three words: "In one year." The poor guy didn't understand. So he repeated again, in broken Spanish: "When do I see you again?" And I repeated, "In one year."

I had to somehow explain to him that I had to go back to Mexico, because I had already signed a contract to start shooting

Rosalinda. I was not exaggerating when I told him that he wouldn't see me for a year, as I had to travel to Mexico the very next day. But he had no idea about the world of Mexican soap operas, and he thought I was just confused, and really meant to say "in one week."

At the moment, neither one of us saw a future. But like the Americans say, "Where there's a will, there's a way." Because I returned to my country and remained locked in the studio for a year and a half, and that still did not stop us from falling in love.

If I was someone who didn't believe in the notion of impossibilities, well, I had finally met someone who felt the same way. When I arrived home, it looked like a flower shop, with cards that said, *It was a pleasure to meet you,* and *I hope to see you soon*—all of them signed by Tommy Mottola.

During one of my calls to thank him for the magnificent floral arrangements and wonderful gesture, he mentioned that he was going to the Caribbean island of St. Barts for a few weeks to spend his vacation on a yacht. So it occurred to me to send him something for his trip: I bought him an amazing pair of sunglasses and a robe for the beach. I went to a friend's store, which had a special sewing machine, had the original label taken off and his name embroidered onto it, and even had his initials sewn onto the front pocket. With both details taken care of, I had the package sent to his office, with a note that read, *This robe is to shield you from the cold when you come out of the ocean, and these glasses are to protect your eyes from the rays of the sun.* Later, he told me that the gifts came as a total shock, because nobody was ever concerned about him, and it was always he who gave, gave and gave. No one had ever stopped to worry about him being cold, or whether his eyes needed protection from the sun. "Aw, baby," he said to me, "you won my heart."

Long-distance Courtship

From the moment that I returned to Mexico, each day more flower arrangements continued to arrive at my house, accompanied by candies, chocolates and teddy bears. We would send each other letters, poems, songs, and that's how we fell in love, like in the old times, when one had to wait months for the letter of a lover who lived far away. But as much as we wanted to do things romantically, retro-style, we were still modern people, which was why at the end of each day, we would always talk until one of us would fall asleep.

Three or four months after our first date, Tommy invited me to spend a weekend with him in Miami. I agreed, because on top of that, Gloria and Emilio wanted to have dinner with us. And as expected, we had a great time, just like family, all very relaxed. We laughed a lot that night. They were happy that their role as Cupid had turned out well. Especially because when they'd told Tommy that I was an actress and a singer, he'd almost stood me up at the restaurant. He had just officially separated and would soon be divorced from Mariah Carey, and the last thing he wanted was to get involved with another singer, and much less an actress—and on top of that, one who didn't even speak his language! But he and I were destined to meet. There was just no way around it.

In fact, when I heard that he was Mariah Carey's ex, I found it funny, because I had no idea who he was until I made that connection. Besides, I had always deeply admired Mariah as a singer. Even more than that: I loved her music. She was a pioneer who showed true innovation with her new vocal style, mostly in ballads, with those high notes that were so unique to her. And, of course, with her manager, who was president of her record label at the time, she was naturally poised to reach the fame that she achieved. Needless to say, now I don't listen to her music so much around the house! But I still think she is a supremely talented woman, worthy of admiration. The most beautiful flower arrangement that I received when my daughter, Sabrina, was born was from her.

At the beginning of the relationship, the rumors about Tommy made me a bit nervous. People said that he was an evil man who kept his women locked up in a "glass cage," and who knows how many other absurdities. They made him out to be like Bluebeard, the classic ogre from horror stories who locked up his wife in the highest, most unreachable tower of the castle. . . . But I was realizing that none of this could possibly be true, because this was not the man I was getting to know, the man I was falling in love with. It was quite the opposite: Tommy was and still is a man among men on every level, and with me he has always been the most dedicated, loving and affectionate husband.

During the year and a half that I spent shooting *Rosalinda,* we continued writing letters to each other; we took photos of ourselves at work and at home; it was like getting to know each other from afar. I would write him, *Look, this is my dressing room; look at my sweet teddy bear; this is what we eat in Mexico.* . . . And I would describe what was in the refrigerator or what was being cooked in my house. I also learned about him from the things he would send: *This is my office; this is what I see every morning; this is my car.* . . . Photo after photo, letter after letter, that was how we kept the flame burning while I finished shooting the soap opera.

After our first meeting in Miami with the Estefans, we thought it would be a good idea to meet there on the weekends. I loved the idea, because the truth is that our love was blooming and what we needed most was to see each other. So I spoke with the producers of my soap opera and told them that I would start shooting much earlier in the morning, if they would let me out at noon on Fridays. The producers already knew me as a "working machine," and knew that if I put my mind to it, I could shoot up to twenty scenes in one take. So they agreed, adding the expected, "That's okay, but take the earliest flight back to Mexico, and come straight to the soundstage, where we will be waiting." There was never any problem. I would leave Televisa and head directly to the airport for the three-hour flight to Miami, which was the same amount of time it would take Tommy to travel from New York. Each Friday I would board a plane, still dressed and made up as Rosalinda, and since I was already showing the early signs of chronic fatigue, I would sleep the whole way. I would ask the flight attendant to wake me up half an hour before the flight landed, so that I could head to the little bathroom, freshen up and change my clothes. When I got off the plane, a car would be waiting to take me directly to the restaurant and, with a martini in hand, my magnate of love.

That was how we spent our first year together as a couple.

When *Rosalinda* finally finished, happy that we could now spend more time together, Tommy invited me to spend the summer with him in his house in the Hamptons. I didn't hesitate for a second, and arrived with two suitcases and my dog. . . . I came as a guest and never went back to Mexico. The truth is that I needed a long vacation. The doctor had told me that because of the workload I had taken on over the last fifteen years, plane after plane, soap after soap, show after show, the physical and emotional wear and tear had taken a toll on my body and I desperately needed to recuperate. I was diagnosed with profound fatigue, lack of sun, and extreme exhaustion so severe that they said I needed a whole year of rest, and who knew whether that would even be enough—I was totally worn-out. So my cure was to include spending the summer in a bikini near a pool, margaritas, dark sunglasses and music. . . . How could I *not* recover like that?

It was during that summer that we fell madly in love. The more time we spent together, the more we liked each other, and the more we liked each other, the deeper we fell in love. At the end of the summer, he said, "Why don't you stay and move in? I want us to live together."

I explained that I promised my mother I'd leave her home dressed in white—in other words, to get married, just like the rest of my sisters . . . a family tradition, and very Mexican. I told him how unlucky I had been in love; whenever I had invested my dreams and bet on love, it never seemed to work. I expressed to him my greatest fear: that I fled from the prospect of marriage not just because I enjoyed my freedom and my fame, but because I was afraid of getting hurt. To take this step toward commitment as a couple, I needed some kind of reassurance.

With great love and patience, Tommy comforted me and convinced me that it would be a great idea. It was as if he'd known me forever, and he knew just what to say to comfort me and help me make up my mind. "Don't be afraid to jump. . . . I'll catch you. My arms will always be outstretched to catch and hold you. Don't be afraid; whatever happens, I will be here. From wherever you jump, I'll catch you. . . . I'll never leave you alone, and I will always be here to hold you." He then continued: "But I want the same for myself; I want to know that I can count on you. . . . You want to jump with me?" Feeling his support and the force of his love for me, I was finally able to release my fears and said, "Why not?"

From that moment on, my life changed completely. Even though I had the great fortune of coming to the United States under the best of circumstances, I was sad to leave my motherland, as I am sure every immigrant must somehow feel. I not only got to experience what it would be like to live my own life, without my mother, but I also began to feel the essence of exile. I am sure a lot of people can relate to me when I say that the yearning for one's motherland is one of the most powerful emotions that a person can feel. It's as if someone pulls from your roots a whole piece of your insides, leaving you with a void that is impossible to fill, the void of the land that watched you grow and filled you with life. It is a feeling that I will have forever . . . for the rest of my life, whether I like it or not.

A Mexican in New York

The hardest thing about being independent is getting started. When I was twenty-eight, full of dreams, fears and hopes, I left Mexico with my life packed up in twelve suitcases to hit the streets of Manhattan. I wanted to live my own fairy tale. I had finally found the man of my dreams, my knight in shining armor. Everything that happened around me was beautiful and very romantic; I had finally found myself at the gates of love.

Unfortunately, my mother wasn't happy when she found out about my marvelous plans. Now, for the first time in her life, she would experience the proverbial empty-nest syndrome; she never lived it when my sisters were married and left the house, because there was always someone with her, and, of course, that someone was me. On top of which, I broke the tradition: I went to live with my lover without being married, deeply troubling my mother, and shattering to pieces her dream of one day being able to see her youngest daughter, all dressed in white, leave the house just as the rest of my sisters had done.

So from living in my hometown, surrounded by the people I love most, I went to share my space every day and for the first time with a man, and moved to the thirty-fifth floor of a Manhattan building that looked like a floating glass box, surrounded by windows on all sides, with a full view of the city. It was as beautiful as it was amazing. But even with everything that my new life in New York had to offer, I deeply missed the familiarity of life in Mexico, just how comfortable and loved I felt when I lived there; living in New York, I felt like I had left behind a part of my very soul. I had to leave my comfort zone that was Mexico, a place where I had it all, to come to New York, where I was just another immigrant, far away from her land. It was a 180-degree change.

It was not the first time that I had lived in the United States. When I was just twenty years old, I bought a house and a convertible in Los Angeles, and I felt that I had already achieved the great American dream. But the experience was totally different. In Los Angeles, it didn't matter where I was; everyone knew me. I felt right at home, from the great restaurants of Beverly Hills and Rodeo Drive to the small, homey Mexican spots where they sold tacos and tamales. That was where I would go to eat with my friends, and all the Mexicans, my countrymen, would come out of the kitchen to say hello. Nothing like New York. New York is an asphalt jungle where competition is rampant; after all, as Frank Sinatra sang: "If I can make it there, I'll make it anywhere. . . ."

In addition to the geographical change, there was also the change of my social environment. From being Thalia, I became the wife of Tommy Mottola. From having all the stares and attention focused on me, now I had to share them with my husband, and especially in New York, where he is a king, and I came along as a faceless queen.

When I would accompany Tommy to some of his charitable functions, I was a total unknown; I would sit at the table that was assigned to us, where the questions would rain down on me with a fury: "And what do you do? Who are you? Where are you from?" And so many times I had to explain who I was, what I did, where I came from . . . something that I never had to do in Mexico, or in any of the places where they knew me and knew the details of my life by heart. It was a radical difference, totally crazy. It was a very stimulating time, but also very difficult.

The change was dramatic: from living a very agitated life with absolutely no days off, I went to a more sedentary lifestyle, one that was comforting in its own way. I made a stop along the road that allowed me to, for the first time in years, find the rest and calm that my body and mind deeply yearned for.

It's one thing to go on vacation to New York, but it is entirely different to live in New York. When Tommy was at work, I would take advantage and see everything I could in this ever-cosmopolitan city. I had all the time in the world to visit museums and galleries, and to admire all the different collections of art, history and archaeology. . . . I saw them all, time and time again. I walked through the streets eating a soft pretzel, or I would get in line to have a hot dog with sauerkraut and a milk shake from Gray's Papaya. . . . These were all things that I'd never had time to enjoy for myself, along with the chance to sit on a bench in Central Park and watch so many people of different ages pass me by, all with different styles, dull or bright colors, with dogs, on bikes, on skates, with their iPods hanging. . . . What diversity, and for the first time I could enjoy these types of moments and simply be one more person among the masses. It was my moment; it was my decision. . . . I finally had the time and space to simply be me.

The first months in New York were about sheer metamorphosis, and my life was changing, like a caterpillar immobilized inside its cocoon until change emerges from the depths of its being, breaking through the shell. The caterpillar begins to extend its wings, regardless of the pain it feels in doing so . . . and finally . . . it frees itself and soars . . . now transformed into a butterfly. It is a painful process, but one of the most beautiful that there is. Just like that caterpillar, I felt so many things changing inside, and soon my moment would come to extend my own wings and reinvent myself. My transformation was on the way.

Both Tommy and I were at our peaks: Tommy was the chairman of Sony Music, with fifteen thousand employees worldwide working beneath him. When he took the job, the company was worth $1 billion. By the time he left, his strategies and performance had increased the company's sales to $7 billion. He was responsible for, among many other concepts, the movement known as the "Latin Explosion," with Shakira, Ricky Martin, Jennifer Lopez and Marc Anthony. He developed the careers of Destiny's Child and Celine Dion, among others.

And on my end, I had become a global brand, my albums and soap operas popular in France, Spain, Turkey, Indonesia, Hungary, Greece, Mexico, Central and South America, to name a few. We had both achieved our professional goals, we were at the pinnacle of our careers and from the professional standpoint, we were completely fulfilled—which is why we were able to focus all our energy on our nascent love.

One of the things that brought us closest together is our passion for music. We would spend hours listening to songs, discussing why we liked them, deconstructing the musical production, the arrangements, the melodies, from both a creative and artistic point of view. From my first album as a solo artist, I have always been involved in even the tiniest details, from how I wanted the guitar to sound, to the synthesizer that I wanted to use, or where I wanted the choruses to come in. I am passionate about writing my songs, and hearing them unfold with my ears.

Lights, costumes, logos and cover art . . . I am always involved in everything. Being a part of the albums' development was always my thing. Thanks to Tommy, I had the good fortune of being at some of the most important album releases of the time. I was the first to hear the first crossover album by Shakira, *Whenever, Wherever*; or the first mix of the track "My Heart Will Go On," interpreted by Celine Dion, and used by the director James Cameron in the film *Titanic*; or to see the latest cut of the video for "Livin' la Vida Loca," by Ricky Martin. When we were watching it, I turned and said to Tommy, "Add more of when he shakes his hips. That's his thing." Being in the studios, meeting the artists, the best composers and producers, from rappers to rockers to pop artists, from Michael Jackson to Bon Jovi—that to me was pure magic. During those moments I was a free spirit, full of lasting arpeggios and constant music.

The Love of My Life

I had never experienced a love like the one I had with Tommy. For the first time I felt that I was with a man in every sense of the word. For the first time I felt free, loving like I never had before; what an amazing feeling of freedom, when love seeps out of your every pore. I was turning into a complete woman, whole and ready to hold on to these warm sentiments in my soul forever, because I knew that I would share my life with Tommy.

In Tommy I found my soul mate. He comes from an Italian neighborhood in the Bronx. Despite being the CEO of the most important record label in the industry worldwide, just like me he comes from a normal, working-class neighborhood. From the moment we were together, whatever was his became mine, and somehow his neighborhood connected me to my own. To this day we buy our meat and bread on the block where the church in which he was baptized is located; my house is always full of breads stuffed with prosciutto and mozzarella. From Dominick's we get pork rinds stuffed with Italian meatballs in red sauce, or we get pastries from De Lillo's, like the cannoli we eat at home with a delicious espresso coffee. Even though I am not in my homeland, the Italian family atmosphere reminds me of my own home—always filled with voices, conversations and that unique sense of warmth that can be felt only among family.

It is amazing to have someone with whom you can speak the same language. In our profession, we have to attend a series of events with many important companies, where we must meticulously keep up with all social etiquette. But when we are alone, our roots come out; in our barrio, we feel comfortable with our jokes, our funky way of talking, our vulgarities, our dark sense of humor—in sum, our authentic selves and the invaluable closeness that brings us together, which is essentially our family.

After living in New York for a while, I knew that I not only wanted to share my life with Tommy, but that I was also able to take the reins of my career and bring it to the United States, where I could likely ride the Latin wave that was turning into an international rage. My mother liked that idea as much as it hurt her. It hurt her even more when I sat down to tell her that it was necessary for our work relationship to end, because I needed to take my career to the next level, but still always counting on her precious advice and observations. But the truth is that what I wanted to do was accomplish my independence and at last enjoy our relationship as mother and daughter.

"You know what, *Mamita?*" I said to her. "I am going to run my career from the United States, and for that I won't need a manager there. I need you to understand me, *Mami*; it is the moment for my crossover and the *Arrasando* project, for which my first English album would be released, entitled *Thalia*; that is the plan that my record label is proposing. Besides, the opportunity also now exists to launch my career as an impresario, selling my line of clothes and accessories in some of the big North American stores. Everything works differently in the United States, with different laws, a different style of accounting and different criteria; everything is different, and neither you nor I understand it now; but I want to learn this on my own . . . firsthand. Please, *Mamita*, understand it is better for me, and it is better for us. I just want to be your daughter. I need my mother."

And with pain on both sides, I broke free.

It was very hard on both of us, as it was a separation of mother and daughter, of two souls who had spent so many years together and shared so much. . . . It was a necessary separation, because that is how life is, because that's what happens when one grows up . . . but that didn't make it any less painful. It took my mother some time to come to terms with my decision, but as with everything in my life and my career, she ultimately understood that this was what I needed and she supported me all the way. I will always be grateful to her for sticking by my side; for our mutual growth and the discovering of an infinite number of beautiful things; for facing, accepting and resolving others; and most of all, for the safety of always being able to count on each other. I will always be grateful for all the times she fought like a warrior to take care of me and protect me, to lobby for me and guard my interests. My mother was, is and will always be the pillar that I grew against, and then I transformed and matured. Honesty, righteousness, sincerity and firmness were values that my mother instilled in me since I was a little girl; there is not and will never be a poem, a song or a phrase, no action that can adequately describe the profound and great love that I feel for her, with all the respect that is owed to the one who gave me life, raised me and loved me unconditionally—my accomplice, my friend. There was such a strong and potent symbiosis between us that if I woke up not feeling well, I would find her also in bed and under the weather. If I felt melancholy or sad, chances were she was to be found in the same state. Even without talking, we understood each other, knew each other, and sensed each other; we didn't even have to utter a single word—we could say it all with a glance. She was one of my greatest loves, the fresh wind that pushes my wings along. Thank you for everything, Mama.

Thanks to this life change, I could finally experience the unequivocal feeling of freedom. Nobody can say they are free until they actually taste it. Many times we think that since we are not held captive or prisoners, that it is synonymous with freedom, but really, I think that if you don't feel freedom from within, you are locked inside your very own prison. I have met so many people who are held captive by their pains, their fears, their problems, the death of a loved one, a certain frustration, a misunderstanding about their way of being—slaves to alcohol, drugs, bad habits, lies, to so many things that, without being conscious of it, they have handed over their precious sense of freedom with which God created us.

The mind is so powerful—it can be your best friend and your worst enemy. A while back I read a book that touched my heart deeply: *What You Say Is What You Get,* by Don Gossett. The author explains how important and transcendent it is to speak only of what is necessary for spiritual growth, and to stop speaking about the innocuous matters that actually diminish the quality of life—kind of like the law of attraction. God gave man a sense of power when He created the verb. . . . His verb, so whatever you pronounce is planted and then grows. Freedom depends on each of us, and we either retain it or we let it go. Everything depends on us. With this lesson, I understood that if there wasn't a change in thinking or speech on my part, it would never fully manifest in my reality or in my very existence.

For example, almost three years ago I found a letter that I had written in 1995, long before I met Tommy. In that letter I had described in detail the exact man that I wanted to have by my side: his appearance, his hands, his legs, everything. . . . I also said that I wanted him to be very loving, dedicated, loyal, committed and fun, exactly as I yearned for him, and many other details that would make him the ideal man for me. What a surprise it was to read the letter years later to discover that it perfectly described that man with whom I now share my life.

What you say is what you get; your words are charged with dynamite.

My story has been written from the beginning of time; God has traced my path. I was able to break down the walls of my own prison, destroy all doubt, end my fears, and decide to take the most important step, which was to face life head-on, outstretch my arms and hold it tight, and I would be able to realize this only on my own, facing life, facing my liberation. I treasured this precious sense of freedom when I discovered it, and today I defend it with all my might from everyone—and mostly from myself.

I learned that freedom depends solely on oneself.

CHAPTER FOUR

LOVE

D_{ear} Love:

I always imagined you as a perfect concept.

The perfect state of being human.

The image I kept in mind was that when I finally enjoyed you, possessed you, I would be able to have infinite joy, the solution to every loss.

There was a constant battle to find you, regardless of time, distance or circumstance.

Throughout history, millions of hearts have sacrificed themselves for you.

How many wars have been unleashed in the name of ideal love?

But you are so fragile and so delicate that if you are not cared for well, you quickly die.

You also know how to be a cold-blooded killer, heartless and meticulous with your victim.

I have had you in full; you have made me vibrate, weep, soar, touch unimaginable universes, feel every atom of my being and discover my most hidden dreams.

And as I walked with you, I encountered some incredible people and some less desirable ones, and only you, Love, with your urges, could control my emotions, and you would trick me and force me to see things that were never actually there.

That's how you brought me along for a good portion of the way, until you and I engaged in a heated conversation in which, with total honesty, I asked you to give me a respite.

We spoke about the lessons that you imparted to me, of what I had learned, of what not to repeat, and about the importance of making mistakes.

And yes, like good friends, we shook hands and promised each other that whenever we meet again, we will first always be good friends, always respectful of each other, accepting each other as we are, without wanting to change each other in any way. We will always be free, natural and honest. Authentic to our essence. We will be like children again: innocent, friendly, simple and soft.

And I live that promise in the here and now.

With my lover, with my children, with my family and my friends.

It is fulfilled with all of them, and all of them fill this list of love that we created on that rainy afternoon.

Now you are in everything and everyone.

Now you live, breathe and shine through me . . . through everything and everyone.

Love

In life, like in love, one must take risks. That's what it is all about. If not, why are we on this planet? I am convinced that the things in life that I take the most risk with are those that have given me the most satisfaction, in my professional and personal lives alike. Love is undoubtedly something that is built over time, that has to be worked on, but if you have never taken a risk and made yourself vulnerable to another person to really give of yourself in full, you will never be able to love in full—because to win, you have to at least bet.

Almost fourteen years ago I took the risk of moving in with a man I'd known for just about one year, interrupted by distance and professional commitments. But my heart was thirsty for the love that he gave me. It felt good, and I thought that if it felt this way, it must be so. So I took a leap into the future, and against the advice of many people around me—including my mother—I went to a new city in a new country to give myself the chance of living out our true love story.

But no matter how in love I may have been, the mind is very powerful. Deep inside my soul, I was not able to quiet the negative thoughts that would come up each day: *You're so stupid! When he is tired of living with you he will leave you high and dry, and he'll never propose because it won't even be necessary, since he already got what he wanted: to have you here in the house. . . .* Even though I knew that Tommy adored me and treated me like a princess, it tortured me to think that these thoughts could become reality; and moreover, my mother repeated them to me every single day. She would say that Tommy was going to humiliate me, and that I was going to end up in bad shape, and very sad. I am sure she didn't say it with malicious intentions, but instead because she cared about me—though I can't say that her warnings didn't affect me. Still, I always responded by saying how happy I was with him, that I knew him and trusted him. I said it so much that she had to believe me, although she kept insisting until right before the wedding.

The Engagement

Shortly after we moved in together, we decided that we wanted to build a house in Miami, because it was clear that we wanted to be together and that at some point we were going to get married. We both knew what was going to happen, because what we were both feeling was just too intense. He always told me that he wanted me to be his wife; he would say it now and again, but I never imagined that he would make his mind up so quickly. One day, without thinking about it, he said to me in a very serious tone, "Let's get married. I love you and I want to spend the rest of my life with you. . . . Let's just get married."

Even though I wanted to hear those words, the emotions that came up at that moment made me instantly cry.

"Tommy, yes, I do want to get married," I answered, all worked up. "But before that, I want something to be perfectly clear between the two of us." I looked steadily into his eyes. "I want you to know that if I'm going to be with you, it will be out of love, and not for anything else. There is a certain pace to my life, and a standard of living. Economically, I am in the position to treat myself to all sorts of luxuries and comforts that I am accustomed to, so whether I'm with you or not, I will always continue to live like this."

"Yes, baby," he said, "I know. That's why the only thing I have to give you is myself. And I want to give you the best of me."

And there, as we hugged and cried, I affirmed in my heart that God was giving me the chance to really live this moment. It was a beautiful conversation and a very important one, but there was no mention of a ring.

A few weekends later, we were on a trip to Miami, where we stayed at the Estefans' house on Star Island, which is where they host their out-of-town guests. There was a beautiful sunset in which the whole sky was tinted purple, accented with sharp streaks of lilac, neon pink and orange. We were watching the final setting of the sun, and he was hugging me from behind as we enjoyed the scenery. We were both dressed to the nines, because we were going to a dinner later on. I told him that it was one of the most precious moments of my life and that I wanted to treasure it in my memory forever. He said, "Really, baby? Hold on for one second," and he was off. Suddenly I was left there by myself, standing like a lone palm tree, just when I had said that it was such a spectacular moment. I didn't understand what had happened to Tommy, and why he left me there, totally abandoned. *He's so odd*, I thought to myself. *What an unusual character.*

Three minutes later he was back and agitated, never losing his sense of gallantry, and with a little present wrapped in silver paper and tied with a small gray satin bow. He put it in my hands very gently, and as he watched me open it, he said, "I want you to always remember this moment that has so deeply moved you." Something told me that it might be my engagement ring. I was overcome with all sorts of nerves and excitement. I was shaking inside, until he mischievously grabbed my ear and in a very romantic tone said, "They're going to look gorgeous on you, really gorgeous."

My longing vanished instantly—I wanted to kill him! And, of course, I said to myself that I shouldn't get my hopes up. Trying to control the lump that had formed in my throat, I untied the knot and started to remove the lovely bow. Gradually I opened the little box, until suddenly, when I saw what was inside . . . I closed it right away. I could not believe what I had just seen! I couldn't believe how beautiful my engagement ring was! Tommy started to cry and said, "Will you marry me?" He placed the ring on my finger, and I was so happy that I almost fainted. We hugged and kissed for a long time, but most of all we cried. We went inside the house, where all our friends were waiting, as Tommy had already told them. It was an amazing dinner celebration, with mojitos, Cuban food, and a couple of tequilas here and there. An incredible night that I will never forget.

We were married six months later. I had found the love of my life, and I guess I felt that time had lost all meaning. Everything was flowing. Even though it was moving very fast, I would not change one iota of my love story. If I could do it all over again, I would do it the exact same way.

I recently remembered something that happened when I was on a trip to New York. It was 1997 and I had gone to promote the release of the animated film *Anastasia*, for which I voiced the lead character and sang the songs for the Spanish release. I was staying at the Plaza Hotel; it was winter and people shuffled in the streets among the Christmas lights and decorations; it was snowing and the snowflakes looked like the stars. From the window of my hotel room, I looked down at the streets laden with people clutching bags filled with Christmas goodies, all that hustle and bustle, that life down there. I thought, *It cannot be that with so many people in the world, I am here alone. How is it possible that my love is not out there? I simply don't believe it.* I said to myself, *My love is out there—I decree it!*

Although I was surrounded by people all day, I felt a profound sense of solitude, a loneliness of the soul. I yearned badly to find the man who would make me feel happy and complete. So that night I decided that when I finally found that person—who, for all intents and purposes, could be walking right down Fifth Avenue— I would walk straight up to him and say, "Hi, love, I have missed you so much." Because I staunchly believe that you actually receive what you intentionally articulate, and that when we want something with all our beings, we are heard. The most amazing thing about this story is that Tommy *was* on those streets; his office was even located near the hotel where I was staying that night. I know that what I said was no coincidence. Without being conscious of it, I had sent him a message, telling him to come and find me when the time was right—and I wanted him to know that I was ready and waiting. He's such an obedient man!

Another amazing moment that confirmed Tommy as the love

of my life was when I learned that he was the manager of Hall & Oates, one of my favorite bands in the history of music. He was not just their manager, but he also sat in the studio and wrote songs with them—the very songs that I always dreamed to, cried to and adored when I was a teenager in Mexico. Tommy had been there since the beginning. He was with me without my ever knowing it, since I was just ten or eleven years old; somehow or other, he was already present in my life.

In all the relationships that I had been in until I met Tommy, I was never really sure of my suitors' true intentions. Most of them got close to me to get something out of it, and very few were honest. Back then, I had already built up a personal defense mechanism, and went so far as to become a very untrusting woman. That was how I went through life until I finally found a man who didn't need anything from me, who loved me for who I am and not for the fame or success that I had achieved; and the same thing happened to him with me. He was a very wealthy businessman at the zenith of his career, and I showed up at the peak of my own success, known all over the world for my soap operas and hit records, and achieved total economic stability. Neither of us was looking to cling to the fame and success of the other; nor did we have any other agenda; we were two hurt and lonely hearts that found each other along the way, and without any prejudices, we began our relationship with the utmost respect and totally open spirits.

In many ways, the key to our success as a couple lies in the fact that by the time we met, we had both already made the mistakes that we needed to make regarding matters of the heart. Wisdom comes from the mistakes of the past, but only if you can acknowledge that you erred. That is the secret: It is when the experience of the bad moments transforms into an invaluable treasure that you can clearly see the path not to follow, and to value instead what is true and real. It has taken me a long time to develop it, but now I have a little antenna that allows me to tune right in to the voice of my intuition.

Tommy and I are on the same level spiritually, emotionally and personally; he is not simply my romantic partner—he is my partner in everything. Even though the years mean nothing, experience is everything. He has also made mistakes, which gives him the serenity to know that he is human, which is why he has a sense of balance that makes me feel secure and calm. His compass is at his center, and in turn, so is mine. How lucky we are to have found each other.

Just like I am in my world, he is a very important figure in the United States, which is why he was embroiled in all sorts of rumors that didn't sit well with me at all. But what matters to me is how Tommy treats me, how I treat him and the very special relationship that we have. Everyone else can imagine whatever they like. What I care about most is that I finally met a man who, like me, clearly knows what he wants. And, even more important, that he knows how to get it . . . and he certainly got *me!*

Mrs. M.

I was on the brink of leaving my singlehood. In a few months I would become Mrs. Mottola, and since I pictured a fairy-tale wedding, there were a lot of detailed preparations to meticulously take care of. All I could think about was the fact that I was getting married, and everything was focused on that moment. My family was with me, imparting advice, supporting me in everything.

Tommy had taken me to Vera Wang, *the* consummate wedding dress designer worldwide, the undisputed number one. Even though she did exquisite work on all of her designs, in my heart I had already decided. More than a great designer, I wanted my dress to be made with a lot of care and love. So I called Mitzy, designer to the stars in Mexico, whom I adore like a brother. I dialed him from my house, and as soon as he picked up, I blurted, "Mitzy . . . I'm getting married."

"Whaaaat?" I heard the scream on the other end of the line.

"Yes! I'm getting married," I repeated, "and there is no one in the world who could make my wedding dress with as much love as you."

It took him about six months to make my dress—it was an absolute dream. It was made with pure silk and organza ordered from import houses in New York and Los Angeles, and was sent to Turkey to be hand-stitched with silver thread, organic pearls and Swarovski crystals. Then the entire ensemble was put together in Mexico. It came out beautifully, albeit very heavy—after the whole thing was finished, it weighed about fourteen kilos (roughly twenty-seven pounds). I also had two other dresses made for that night: one for the wedding dinner, monogrammed TMT, for Thalia and Thomas Mottola, and a lighter one in which I could dance the night away.

Tommy and I decided to spend the night before the wedding apart. Even though we lived under the same roof, I wanted to spend that night with my family, and pictured myself leaving my house dressed in white, although in this case my house was the Mark Hotel in Manhattan. Even so, Tommy and I got together for our last unmarried day, because it was very important for me that we say a prayer together and that he accept Jesus into his heart; Jesus had to be the head figure who would stand before our marriage. Together we prayed and connected spiritually, and it was a truly beautiful moment. In fact, that was our real moment of union, because we were standing before God.

The next day, December 2, 2000, everything was crazy. All my sisters, my mother and my grandmother were each in different rooms, running from one to another, since they each had their own makeup artists and hairdressers, while my friends from Mexico finished dolling up to the absolute maximum. Everything was going perfectly fine until I looked in the mirror and—oh, surprise—noticed the gigantic pimple that had emerged right above my cheek. I couldn't believe it! How could I possibly get a *fucking* pimple on the day of my wedding? It would have been tragic if it hadn't been so funny. Fortunately, my ever-talented makeup artist managed to hide it as much as possible, and besides, it was probably stress that caused it in the first place. It was Murphy's Law in full swing!

Everything was going smoothly until I heard a voice in a tone that I didn't like one bit.

"My Thalia . . ." Mitzy said nervously, his voice as fragile as a tiny little thread, "your wedding dress does not fit inside the elevator."

What was he talking about? What did he mean, my wedding dress didn't fit? I entered into full bridezilla mode: Where would I put it on? How would I leave the hotel? I had to put it on somewhere. Right away we called the manager of the hotel and he lent me one of the party rooms on the first floor. Among tables, chairs and furniture, Mitzy and his assistant, Daniel, who had also been a part of my family all my life, proceeded to dress me. They worked tirelessly to make sure the dress hung on me just the right way, and it seemed that everything had been solved, until we stepped out of the hotel to get into the limousine and discovered—as everyone stood there in disbelief—that there was no way for me to get inside. It was ridiculous. The dress was so big it didn't even fit through the car door!

"Dani!" I said, almost screaming. "Get in first and pull the train of the dress."

The scene was worthy of a Cantinflas movie: Mitzy and Daniel piled themselves into the limo and managed to bring the yards and yards of dress into the car folding it in a way so that when I got out, the train of the dress would gradually unfold itself. My mom got in next to help with the dress's crinoline, and I was the last one to get in. *Never say never!* I said to myself. *You can fit anything into a tiny jar; it's just a question of knowing how to accommodate things.* But the truth is that this was no jar—it was one of the largest, most ample limousines that we could find in the state of New York.

The ceremony was set to take place in St. Patrick's Cathedral, located on Fifth Avenue. The curious thing about this story is that when I was fourteen and went on a trip to New York with my mother, when we went to visit the cathedral and sat on one of the wooden pews near the altar, I looked at her and said, "I will get married here someday." I didn't remember this until I was in the middle of planning my wedding and my mother reminded me. The law of attraction really is incredible. . . . How could I know at age fourteen whom I would marry or where? It thrills me to think that everything we do, say or live is all part of a perfect plan.

A week earlier, Catherine Zeta-Jones and Michael Douglas had been married nearby. The New York Police Department had to block off the avenue for security reasons, because there were about three thousand people who had come to watch the affair. Can you imagine three thousand people sharing one of the most important days of your life? I was amazed. I was even more amazed when I later found out that on the day of my wedding, close to ten thousand people came to accompany us on such a special date. There were people there from all over the world—from the Philippines, Mexico, Greece and all of Latin America. I was moved and humbled by such an extraordinary display of affection, and to this day I am thankful to the many fans who came to celebrate and be a part of my own personal fairy tale. Who would have imagined that a little girl from Mexico City would end up getting married in such a beautiful place, surrounded by fans, friends and family from all around the world? It was such a blessing, something that I will always remember and carry in my heart.

Right before we arrived at the cathedral, I suddenly felt something at my feet. I couldn't even see Daniel or Mitzy, since the dress practically took up all the space in the limousine.

"Mitzy!" I yelped. "Something is all tangled up at my feet; I can't move them. Someone doesn't want me to get married. . . . Someone doesn't want me to get married!"

Dani immediately kicked into high gear and practically nose-dived beneath the many layers of fabric to get to my feet.

"I don't see a thing; turn the light on, or give me a flashlight or something," he said, all flustered.

Where did he think we were going to find a flashlight? The four of us were acting like crazy people in the car, while everyone outside waited for Thalia to come out in all her splendor, the very picture of a princess marrying her knight in shining armor. But Thalia was about to have a panic attack. The driver of the limo pulled out a flashlight from God knows where, which somehow got to Dani from one hand to the next. We held a nervous silence for a couple of minutes, when suddenly a voice emerged from the depths of all that fabric. "I see it! You're tangled up in one of the threads that came from the crinoline," he explained as he trimmed the renegade thread, mending the "small problem." Everything happened so fast. . . . Suddenly I felt that my ankles were being liberated just a few meters from where the limousine was going to stop at St. Patrick's Cathedral.

When the limo arrived, Emilio Estefan and my sister Laura, who were the sponsors of the wedding, were already waiting for me; my family was there as well. I exited the car without any trouble in front of thousands upon thousands of flashes that bombarded me at the same time. Screams of jubilation accompanied every move that I made, and the excitement of seeing all those thousands of people brought tears to my eyes. I had to control myself so that I wouldn't cry from being so moved. As I ascended the huge steps of the cathedral, the massive train of the dress covered them all.

Tommy and I had decided that we wanted an intimate ceremony with just our family and friends, so as soon as we walked in, the doors of the church were closed. We wanted to film the ceremony, and we wanted to do it ourselves. A camera was set up on a crane to capture everything, along with three additional cameras placed strategically around the cathedral, which would cover the entire ceremony. It was practically like a television special that Tommy wanted to shoot—but just for us. All the paparazzi were left outside during the ceremony. In fact, prior to the event, a team of security agents came into the church to ensure that everything was in order, and they discovered a photographer who had climbed up one of the columns. How many hours could he have possibly lingered up there at the top of that column? I have no idea, but they brought him down and showed him to the exit.

I was in a small room when the ceremony began. Watching in

the reflection, I could watch my sisters walk in, and then my mother, and my heart wanted to leap out of my chest . . . what a special and unique moment. When I heard the first chords of the wedding march, I started walking toward the altar.

I had asked for my dress to have a very long train, which would be attached at the waist and then taken off after the ceremony. I wanted it to represent everything that I had experienced and lived through up to that moment, everything that I carried with me: the doubts, the losses, the loneliness, the sadness, the terrors and the fears. The wedding was the moment to release it all, to leave the past behind and to free myself up to the beautiful present that was opening itself up to me. Everything was going fine until I got to the steps leading up to the altar and found I had trouble moving forward; of course—I hadn't considered the rug that covered that small staircase, and now the pearls, Swarovski crystals and silver threads were getting trapped by the fibers of the rug. Every step that I took was a real effort, the dress was just so heavy, until I finally reached my destination, right beside my future husband.

Now that I think about it, I don't know whether I even re-alized everything I carried in my heart, and that I was on the brink of releasing it all in that moment. Suddenly, standing there at the altar with the love of my life, I turned around and saw my sisters, my mother, my grandmother, my family and friends sitting in the front row, all of them witnesses to various moments of my life, growing with me and accompanying me, and now delivering me to the man who had won my heart, all of them sharing in my joy.

When the ceremony ended, the train of my dress was re-moved, and I could finally move around more freely. Yes . . . I had shed the past and was now ready to face the present and the future. Elated, my distinguished husband and I held hands, and on our way out we again heard people screaming in every language, all wishing us well. It was beautiful. How can I pay back these outward displays of love? They really are priceless.

We arrived at the reception hall, which was decorated stunningly, to greet our five hundred guests, the Mexican and Spanish-speaking friends mostly on one side of the room, and the Americans on the other side. Well, cliques will form anywhere! The big surprise of the night came when the lights were turned off and the silence was broken by Donna Summer singing the first words of "Last Dance." It was the gift of all gifts for me, as she has always been one of my favorite artists. The minute she appeared on the stage, everyone went right to the dance floor and started singing and dancing to the beat of those notes. When we were even more lit up, Emilio Estefan went up on the small stage and played the bongos, while his wife, Gloria, sang with Marc Anthony, and one of my nephews played guitar. Later, Tommy and I went up, along with the comedienne Rosie O'Donnell, all singing and playing together. From the stage I could see Jennifer Lopez, Danny DeVito, Cristina Saralegui and Lili Estefan dancing, and, sitting a bit farther away, Michael Jackson, Robert De Niro and Bruce Springsteen, among others. What a sight! Never in my wildest dreams would I have ever imagined that one day I would be celebrating my wedding alongside so many of these extraordinary artists I have admired my entire life. At some point during the night Tommy sat me in a chair close to the dance floor, grabbed the microphone and began to sing Frank Sinatra's "I've Got You Under My Skin." It was a beautiful moment, because I knew that he would always hold me very close, deep inside, in his being, under his skin.

As in "Cinderella," at twelve midnight the Americans got up and left. I thought to myself, *What?! The party is just starting!* But all Latinos have some kind of superbattery, and the Mexican guests said, "So, what time is the *pozolazo*, Thali?" because in Mexico not only is there the wedding dinner, but when it is almost dawn, we serve a delicious *pozole* (traditional Mexican soup), nice and spicy to keep people awake and festive. That was a little piece of my country, right there in the heart of Manhattan.

I had already planned all my outfits and everything seemed sorted out. But when Tommy and I decided to "flee," it suddenly occurred to us that I would need something with which to cover up on the way out. My third dress was very light, and since it was December, the outside temperature was below zero. If I had walked out like that I would have frozen! So I gave a quick look around and saw my nephew's wife wearing a brown fur coat, probably fox. I went right over to where she was standing and practically took it off her, saying, "I'll send it to the hotel to-morrow," and with the fur thrown over my shoulders, we vanished from the scene. Tommy and I were on our way to our honeymoon.

Marriage and Family

As in every marriage, Tommy and I adjusted to our new life, sharing everything and making decisions together. Cohabiting is day-to-day work, and building and strengthening our relationship, planning every step and every idea, has been a constant learning experience for both of us. Discovering our limits and where we can reach without violating the other person's personal space is a whole new challenge, a wonderful challenge that has allowed us to mature as a married couple and as people.

After the wedding, I continued to work on my projects. I continued to work on my album *Arrasando,* and concert tours, along with *Thalia,* the English album, and the single with Fat Joe. I developed a clothing line for Kmart, a line of chocolate with Hershey's, a collection of glasses and sunglasses at Kenmark Optical, and I can say that all of this kept me quite busy.

Ultimately, it is part of my upbringing. In my house, most of my sisters worked; it was part of our worldview: "Forward ever, backward never," as my song says. So I kept on doing what I knew: working, while growing alongside my husband, who, despite being a bit older than me, shares with me a perpetual adolescence. Our age difference was actually quite normal to me, since my mother had also married a man who was a lot older than her, and in turn, so did my sisters. In fact, the youngest of my brothers-in-law is ten years older than my sister, and the oldest is twenty-two years older—which is why it has always been normal for me to have an older man by my side. It is part of the history of the women in my family.

Selecting a father for my children had always been a subject that terrified me. I was afraid that he wouldn't be good enough or that he wouldn't be devoted to his kids; I was afraid that something would happen to him, or that he would die like my father. After a few years of being married, I thought that it was time to have a baby; besides, my biological clock was starting to tick. When we began to plan the arrival of the baby, I realized that Tommy was as much of a neophyte as me, despite having had two children with his first wife. What happened was that he had given himself so fully to his career for all those years that he missed the best moments of the first years of his kids' life. We were basically two people wanting to be parents, but lacking any experience.

When the desire to have a baby came into my mind, the obsessive thinking patterns came back. I was scared that I would not be ready for such a monumental challenge. The contradictory thoughts spun circles in my mind. *What if I am not a good mother?*

I thought. *I don't want to repeat the behavior patterns of my own home. . . . And what if Tommy and I are not good parents?* A storm of crazy ideas flushed my mind at a thousand miles per hour, and all I could think was that I didn't want to repeat any of my family patterns, much less for Tommy to do so. I was convinced that both of us needed to find a way to give our children the necessary time to grow up happy and confident, and not allow work to take priority over our family's needs. We would give ourselves the assignment of finding the exact balance, where work would never impose on family.

I also made sure to be fair with Tommy and to not judge him for his past as a father, because all human beings have the power to change, and not only have the right, but also the ability to become better people each day. He was dying to be a father again, and that was the only thing that I needed to take into consideration. In my own present, I had found the man who would be my partner for life. Tommy was the man whom I had always dreamed of being with, the father I always wanted to give to my kids.

Still, like everything in life, things don't always turn out the way we plan them. When we finally decided that we were ready to conceive, we were not able to. We began trying in 2004, and if there is anything that I regret, it is not having tried to have children sooner after we were married, because it was very hard for me to become pregnant. Nobody tells you that after the age of thirty, a woman starts to produce fewer healthy, fertilizable eggs. And after age thirty-five, a woman gets pregnant only if she is lucky, because women are born with a finite number of eggs that gradually die over the years. On top of that, society says, "Be successful and fulfill yourself professionally first, because later you will have time to have children." How many of us fall into this trap and later regret it because our bodies are no longer strong enough to handle a pregnancy? And in some cases, this starts at home, from our very own mothers and grandmothers, who didn't have another option but to stay home and start breeding at the age of sixteen, and seeing us, who have other options, advise us to not make the same "mistake" they made. In my particular case, with a body that was already so exhausted from all the coming and going, sleepless nights, flights, time changes and obligatory work, getting pregnant would be an uphill battle.

The fact that it was hard for me to get pregnant was tough on Tommy, too, mostly because he could not avoid thinking that maybe life was paying him back for not being present with Sarah and Michael, his kids from his first marriage. He conceived them, and they are his children, but in reality he was never with them as much as a parent should be because he was too busy being Tommy Mottola, worldwide impresario. He became obsessed with his work and that's how he spent his days, and his kids' lives totally passed him by. When we talked about this subject, he would always say, "*Baby*, you don't know how much I have suffered knowing that I missed their most important years, that I wasn't there to support them during their most vulnerable moments. And the worst part about it is that I can't turn the page back, no matter how badly I want to. I try to be a better father now and help them with everything, but they already see me as a distant parent." From my end of it, I can see how desperate he is to be present in their lives, but you can't turn back time, and the three of them have been deeply affected by what happened. I felt that having a baby would be a way to also give the three of them the chance to reconnect and salvage the relationship as father and children, in the face of a new perspective, and I knew that it would give Tommy a second chance to do it right.

And for me, it was a lot of pressure to think, *Why did I wait so long to have children? I have been so egotistical!* But everything has its payback, and patience is indeed a virtue. While we struggled and gambled on life, destiny held a very special surprise for us that would not only test our love as a couple, but it would also engage the love of an entire family with an event that would radically change our lives. Once again, love would be the backbone that would hold us together during this difficult period and, at the end of it all, allow us to look back with more perspective. Love took charge and love prevailed.

Love, with its compassionate strings, with its great amount of patience, with its wisdom, wove a net with which to rescue us and restore our hearts, which at the time had crumbled against the pressure we had to endure. If it hadn't been that way, we would have given up at the first attempt, instead of celebrating every day the great victory that is the gift of life.

CHAPTER FIVE

FORGIVENESS

D_{ear} Forgiveness:

How many times have you passed by and spoken with my heart?

How many times have you wanted to take me by the hand and walk with me? I honestly don't know.

You have never ceased to insist; you have been knocking on my door ever since I was a little girl; sometimes we walked together, and sometimes I never even opened the door.

But today I understand that you are a part of me.

Your love, patience, tenacity and insights have caused me to understand how important it is to release the blinders that have precluded me from seeing things with clarity and sincerity.

Thanks to you, I have been able to find balance in my life.

Thanks to you, I have recovered, and have forgiven what has caused me harm; I have forgiven a lot of people, close and far, known and unknown, loved or liked, who one way or another have hurt me throughout the course of life; and the most important thing is that you, my beloved Forgiveness, have taught me to rediscover myself and to accept myself as I am.

I will never let you leave my side.

All I ask is that you continue to walk with me.

With your help, I will be able to face anything.

I will be able to see with your eyes, so that I can forgive even that which I don't necessarily understand, and let it go.

Forgiveness, the older brother of Freedom . . . thank you for standing by my side.

Forgiveness

Accepting my mistakes has been a crucial step in the journey of my spiritual growth. It has not been easy for me to learn how to forgive, mostly to forgive myself. Even more than that, if it had not been for my sister Ernestina, with whom I saw the most precious and absolute example of forgiveness, perhaps I would never have been able to accomplish it.

The night of September 22, 2002, my life and my family's life changed forever. That day my sisters Laura and Ernestina were kidnapped. This horrific event is and has always been one of the greatest traumas and one of the experiences that has been hardest for me to overcome. I could not forgive myself for the fact that being in the public eye, and married to someone like Tommy, a pivotal figure in his industry, had caused someone to steal my sisters' freedom. It is in large part because of that, out of respect for the privacy of my sisters, and keeping in mind how delicate and complicated the situation is, that I have never publicly spoken about this matter. However, I cannot speak about my life, about the process that I have endured to rediscover myself, to accept myself and find my balance, without talking about how I lived through that terrible time. Because I can say without a doubt that it is the greatest test that God has ever placed before me. Only forgiveness has allowed me to overcome this event, which paralyzed us, and taught me how to live with the massive pain that I still feel every time I think of those thirty-four hellish days. Because even though it was my two sisters who were physically kidnapped, emotionally the entire family was held hostage; all the old fears, pains and wounds of the past came to the surface, along with the anguish of not knowing how the whole ordeal would play out.

The twenty-second of September, 2002, had unfolded like any other day, and night was beginning to fall. After I had a massage, I went up to my room to get ready for bed, when I received a phone call: "*Bueno* . . ." I answered, as always. On the other end of the line I heard, "Is this Thalia?" I didn't recognize the voice, which was why I knew right away that something was not right. Nobody calls my house asking for Thalia, because no one who knows me calls me by my stage name. I even thought that maybe it was a fan who'd somehow gotten hold of my phone number and wanted some kind of personal information, so I asked him to please not disturb us, and was about to hang up when he added, "You don't know me, but I am a friend of your sisters' and I have them captive. So you know, I have them in my control, and I am calling you because I got your number from their cell phones. I have them with me, under my control, these two old broads. . . ."

Before I allowed myself to keep listening, I told him to stop bothering us and quickly hung up the phone. I went running downstairs to Tommy and told him what happened. He tried to calm me down, but I could see the fear in his eyes. Although I didn't want to believe what I had just heard, deep inside I knew that this voice had been telling the truth. I felt it intuitively; I could sense it; there was no question about it; my mind would try to negate it, but deep in my heart I knew it was true. I felt a strange rush of adrenaline, an unbearable sense of anxiety.

I immediately called my sister Laura's house, and her eldest son answered the phone.

"My love, where is your mother?" I asked.

His voice sounded terrified when he responded, "*Tía*, someone just called to tell me that my mom and Aunt Titi have been kidnapped."

At that moment I was completely taken over by an avalanche of fear, anguish, terror, pain and helplessness, the kind of desperation that does not allow you to move or to think. I had the urge to run and scream all over the place, to pull my hair out and yank off my own skin. Whom do you turn to? Whom do you ask for help? Who can console your heart in these moments? At that point we knew it was not some kind of tasteless prank. Laura and Titi had been kidnapped. I could not believe it. My head was spinning and I went into a state of shock. One of the things that most affected me was that everything was happening in Mexico and I was in New York, which only served to heighten that awful sense of helplessness.

I had been involved in three serious car accidents that, without God's help, I might have not survived. That recurring sensation of "What just happened?" that comes up when your present is interrupted by something catastrophic was very familiar. It is practically a head-on collision, a crash that you don't expect, a calamity that you don't perceive as coming imminently

toward you, and what results is the feeling of a surreal reality—
which is exactly what I felt the night that I received that call.

I instantly thought about my sisters, about how they must be
doing, wondering whether they were injured, whether they had
been hurt. I thought of how they must be alone, at the mercy of
God knew who, afraid, thinking about their children, their families. The only thought that went in circles through my mind was,
How can I help? God, what helplessness, what pain and what
solitude. And my nephews and nieces, Laura's and Titi's kids, how
were they? The feeling of being orphans . . . All I wanted to do was
hug them tight and assure them that all of this would pass and
that everything would be okay. I knew that my mother would go
completely crazy when she found out, and just thinking about
that broke my heart. What a difficult moment . . . so much pain,
such anxiety, and me in New York, so far away from my country,
from my family, from everything.

I felt terribly lost. An absolute fear takes over my entire soul
when I think back to that day, and I can say that it has been a very
long process to come to accept, to understand and digest everything about that pain in order to move forward. Regardless of how
many people have to endure this on a daily basis, it feels as though
one is the only person and the only family who has ever been
through it. Still, you know that there are other human beings who
have gone through exactly what you are experiencing at that
moment, and what is important to eventually understand is that
no one carries the blame for what happened; it is simply something that had to happen. For a long time, I tortured and blamed
myself for everything that my sisters went through, until I finally
understood, after a lot of work, that all of it is really out of my
hands, because ultimately it is all in the hands of God. That is
how I learned to release all that pain, that helplessness, that load,

that guilt, from the depths of my heart, to be able to recover my peace and my sense of balance.

The Kidnapping

The night of the kidnapping, Titi was going to watch Laura act in the play *The House of Bernarda Alba*. Titi was the sister who is always ready to support the others, but that night she had no desire to go to the theater. It was Sunday, and, in fact, her hip was hurting, so she was already in bed. One of her daughters had gotten hold of tickets to see the play with her boyfriend and his parents, but they ultimately decided to go somewhere else. So they had several tickets that were going to go to waste, and when Titi got a call from her friend Ana, who said she and her husband would like to go, she agreed to go along. She got out of bed, got herself ready and waited for them to pick her up.

So they went and saw the play, and at the end they said hello to Laura, and she suggested they all go to a café that was located near the theater.

But unfortunately, they never arrived. When they were on their way—Laura and Ernestina were in the same car—a garbage truck crossed their path suspiciously, blocking traffic along the avenue, leaving only one space for a car to pass, and when they turned around, the kidnappers were already waiting. That was the moment that our interminable nightmare began.

What happened to us as a family has sadly happened to thousands of people in Mexico and all over the world. The wounds left by the experience of a kidnapping are deep, and sometimes incurable. My sister Titi, being a writer, wrote a book called *Líbranos del Mal* (*Deliver Us from Evil*) as a form of catharsis to heal her soul. There she gives the full account of what she endured, because even though it is the same story, every member of the family lived through their own particular and personal version of it. In fact, even Laura's and Titi's experiences were different, as each one lived it from her own unique perspective. Because everyone is different, and everyone has their own way of dealing with and understanding what they experience. Laura wrote a play entitled *Cautivas* (*Captive*), in which she also found her own form of catharsis to heal her soul. Both *Líbranos del Mal* and *Cautivas* share the pain and helplessness that is felt, and the uncertainty of knowing that your destiny and your life lie in the hands of a total stranger. But the works differ insofar as the personal experience that they each relay, as each one depicts it from her point of view, based on her own perspective of the experience, from the emotions that each one felt at that moment, which, despite being very intense and similar feelings, were processed differently and handled based on each woman's own character and personality.

Once in the house where they would endure the kidnapping, they had only each other, and when one of them shivered in fear, the other one would console, and when one cried, the other would try to calm her down. There was a list of very strict rules that they were instructed to obey, like covering their faces, mostly their eyes, when the kidnappers would knock on the door to give them their plates of food, so that they would not be able to look their kidnappers directly in the face. They were held together in a small room that had a tiny bathroom in it.

Meanwhile, outside everyone reacted in their own way: My mother suffered panic attacks and tachycardia, landing in the hospital on one occasion, and having to be treated in her car because she was surrounded by reporters who were hunting for news. One time, my grandmother saw a dramatization on a television special and suffered a panic and anxiety attack that caused her to run around the house screaming like crazy, until she fell and hurt herself badly. When she heard the news about the kidnapping, Titi's oldest daughter fainted, and every time she would regain consciousness, she would faint all over again—she simply could not process what was happening. All the while, the negotiations continued. Needless to say, negotiating is a very exhausting process that takes time. Sometimes it takes years, sometimes months and other times weeks. Unfortunately, there is no rule or criteria for how things are supposed to go, or how long things are supposed to take: It all depends on the parties involved, both on the side of the victims' families, and on the kidnappers themselves.

Even though it seems paradoxical, the kidnappers continued to threaten my sisters, but they also took care of them. What I do know is that during the entire time that they were held hostage, the kidnappers struggled to chip away at their fortitude and pushed them to terror, and my sisters did not know what would become of their lives, asking themselves each day whether it would be their last. During all the days of their captivity, the television and radio were blasting at full volume, while the kidnappers—between screams and loud words—provoked in my sisters a constant state of total instability and sheer terror.

After sixteen days of captivity, and because both parties had reached a monetary agreement, the kidnappers gave my sisters the option of choosing whom they would set free first. Their strategy was to let one of my sisters go so that she would tell the world all the atrocities they had endured so that we would make sure to give them whatever the kidnappers asked for.

The one who was released was Laura; Titi stayed. She who

was at home in her pajamas on that Sunday night, who accompanied her friends so that they wouldn't have to go alone, who simply had no real reason for being there that night. The kidnappers already had their sights on Laura, and now they had them both. Maybe it was providence that allowed Titi to be there that night with Laura, and maybe Laura would not have come out of it alive had Titi not been there. Maybe the damage would have been even greater. We will never know what would have happened—but I do know that we were very lucky.

From the moment she was set free, Laura was fervently determined to rescue Titi by any means necessary. She immediately told us about the state that Titi was in, and what the kidnappers were going to do if we did not comply with their demands. From that instant, we moved as fast as possible to try to save Titi.

Unfortunately, those last sixteen days that Titi endured in captivity were the most terrifying. The kidnappers started to lose their patience, because collecting the ransom was taking too long—without acknowledging, of course, how much the media held us up with their commentary about the whole thing—and they decided they were going to mutilate my sister and send us a piece of her body as one final threat. Fortunately, one of the gang leaders prevented the mutilation and saved her finger . . . because he'd fallen hopelessly in love with her. It was obviously not real love, but rather what is known as Stockholm syndrome, only in reverse. Stockholm syndrome is a physical reaction in which a prisoner comes to identify with his or her captor. In this case, the one who fell in love was the captor himself, who somehow clung to my sister.

Titi and I have talked a lot about this horrifying ordeal. During one of our chats she mentioned that the thoughts she clung to were: *I have to see my daughters again; I have to see my family. God,*

Mi madre y mi padre en Xochimilco. / My mom and my dad in Xochimilco.

Esta es "la Chancha" como le llamábamos en casa a esta cabeza reducida. / This is "la Chancha," the nickname we gave this tiny head at home.

La Reducción de Cabezas es el "Hobby" de un Científico

Mi padre y yo. / My father and I.

Saliendo de mi casa, arriba izquierda, rumbo al Kiosco Morisco. / On my way out to the Kiosco Morisco.

En La Paz, Baja California. Una autentica mini-Marimar. / In La Paz, Baja California. An authentic mini-Marimar.

En mi escuelita con mi madre. / At preschool with my mother.

Mi bautizo en los brazos de mi madre con todas mis hermanas. / My baptism in the arms of my mother, with all my sisters.

El programa de televisión, *La Mujer Ahora*. / The TV show *La Mujer Ahora*.

La primera vez que salí en televisión cuando tenía 3 años. / My first appearance on TV at three years old.

Mi sección de cocina con Eve-lyn la Puente show matutino. / My cooking segment on Evelyn la Puente's morning show.

Primera vez intrepretando a Sandy en *Vaselina* junto con Benny Ibarra como Danny. / The first time I played Sandy in *Grease* with Benny Ibarra in the role of Danny.

Timbiriche. / The band Timbiriche.

En el papel de María la del Barrio en el basurero. / In my character María la del Barrio standing in a real landfill.

Cantando en una presentación de Timbiriche. / Singing at a Timbiriche show.

Uno de los looks de mi disco *Love* hecho con margaritas, mis favoritas. / One of my looks for the *Love* album, made with daisies, my favorite flower.

Una de mis presentaciones en *Siempre en Domingo* conducido por Raul Velasco. / One of my performances on *Siempre en Domingo*, hosted by Raul Velasco.

Los vestuarios excéntricos han sido parte de casi toda mi carrera. / Eccentric wardrobes have always been a huge part of my career.

En el pico mas alto de populari-
dad de la trilogía de las Marías,
yo visito Las Filipinas. Las novelas rompieron records de audien-
cia en 180 países y han sido vistas
por dos mil millones de personas
en el mundo. / At the height of
the popularity of the novela trilogy, I visited Manila, Phillipines.
The novelas were highly rated and
seen in more than 180 countries
by more than two billion people.

María Mercedes. / María Mercedes.

Marimar. / Marimar.

Adela Noriega y yo en *Quinceañera*. / Adela Noriega
and I in *Quinceañera*.

Renacimiento como intérprete, *Primera fila* en vivo. / Comeback as a perfomer during *Primera fila*, live.

Premio lo Nuestro a la Música Latina. / Lo Nuestro Award for Latin Music.

Celebrando las ventas de "Piel Morena" y "Amor a la Mexicana". / Celebrating the sales of "Piel Morena" and "Amor a la Mexicana".

Músicos en recepción con gobernadores de Bali. / Musicians during a reception with the governor of Bali.

Donde viajo celebran mi nacionalidad con un buen mariachi. ¡Viva México! / Wherever I go, my nationality is celebrated with a good Mariachi band. *¡Viva México!*

Recepciones tipicas de cada país con sus vestuarios, y siempre rodeada de los niños. / Typical receptions in the countries I've visited, typical clothes, and always surrounded by children.

Reflejando una profunda triztesa en Venecia. Ni la juventud, ni los jóvenes guapos llenaban mi soledad. / Looking very sad in Venice. Neither my youth nor the good-looking boys could fill my solitude.

Visitando un orfelinato en México D.F. 2001. / Visiting an orphanage in Mexico City in 2001.

Como la portavoz de March of Dimes in 2006. / My job as the spokesperson for the March of Dimes in 2006.

Reunión con fans en Europa 2005. / Meeting my European fans in 2005.

Vistiéndome en el salón de fiestas del Hotel Mark. / Getting dressed at Hotel Mark in New York.

En la limusina camino a mi boda. Derecha a mi madre, Mitzy, y en la mano izquierda Danny. / In the limo on my way to my wedding ceremony. My mother and Mitzy to the right, Danny on the left.

Cortando nuestro pastel de bodas. Cada piso era un sabor diferente. / Cutting our wedding cake. Every level had a different flavor.

Tommy y yo con Michael Jackson el día de mi boda. / Tommy and I with Michael Jackson on our wedding day.

Gloria Estefan y Rosie O'Donnell suben al escenario mientras Donna Summers canta en nuestra boda. / Gloria Estefan and Rosie O'Donnell hop onstage as Donna Summers sings at our wedding.

Tommy y yo con Gloria y Emilio Estefan. / Tommy and I with Gloria and Emilio Estefan.

Presentación navideña en Rockefeller Center al otro lado de la catedral de San Patricio donde Tommy y yo nos casamos. / A Christmas special performing on Rockefeller Plaza across from St. Patrick's Cathedral, where Tommy and I got married.

Bailando con el Presidente Barack Obama durante el concierto de "In the White House: Fiesta Latina", celebrando la herencia musical hispana en el South Lawn de la Casa Blanca, octubre 13, 2009. / Dancing with President Barack Obama during the "In Performance at the White House: Fiesta Latina" concert, celebrating Hispanic musical heritage, on the South Lawn of the White House, October 13, 2009.

El final del concierto en la Casa Blanca el 13 de octubre durante la grabación de "In Performance at the White House: Fiesta Latina." De izquierda a derecha: Eva Longoria, George Lopez, Tito "El Bambino", Marc Anthony, Jennifer Lopez, Gloria Estefan, Emilio Estefan, José Feliciano, yo y miembro de Aventura Anthony "Romeo" Santos. / The concert finale at the White House of the October 13 taping for "In Performance at the White House: Fiesta Latina": (*left to right*) Eva Longoria, George Lopez, Tito "El Bambino," Marc Anthony, Jennifer Lopez, Gloria Estefan, Emilio Estefan, José Feliciano, me, and Aventura member Anthony "Romeo" Santos.

Tommy y yo en una barbacoa para el 4 de julio en Aspen. / Tommy and I at a Fourth of July BBQ in Aspen.

¡Mi primera pesca! Montauk, N.Y. / My first catch! Montauk, New York.

Escalando en Utah. / Rock climbing in Utah.

Clases de trapecio en Bridgehampton, verano de 2010. / Trapeze lessons in Bridgehampton, summer 2010.

Mi cumpleaños en Da Silvano, dos meses antes de que naciera Sabrina. ¡Tommy me sorprendió con un pastel especial! / My birthday at Da Silvano, two months before Sabrina was born. Tommy surprised me with my likeness on the birthday cake.

Recogiendo manzanas en Millbrook, N.Y. Este es posiblemente el momento en el que contraje la enfermedad del Lyme. Es una zona muy bella, con muchos árboles ¡y muchas garrapatas! / Picking apples at the orchard in Millbrook, New York. This is possibly the moment I could have contracted Lyme disease. The area is beautiful but heavily wooded and full of deer ticks!

Último mes de medicinas y suplementos prescritos para combatir el Lyme. / Last month of medicines and supplements prescribed for my Lyme disease.

Perdiendo mi pelo y mi masa muscular en la lucha contra la enfermedad de Lyme. / Losing my hair and muscle mass in the fight with Lyme disease.

Sabrina y yo. / Sabrina and I.

JIMMY IENNER JR.

Mis dos amores: Sabrina cantándole a su hermanito en mi pancita, le dice "Yuyu". / Here are my two loves. Sabrina is singing to her baby brother in my belly, whom at the time she called "Yuyu."

COURTESY OF THE AUTHOR

please grant me the wisdom to handle this with tenacity; give me the necessary calm to not lose my mind.

"This is why I am sitting here with you, holding your hand and talking with you," she explained to me.

I said to her, "Sister, I am certain that only the strongest of souls can live through such an ordeal, and I think it allows you to reach higher spiritual levels than everyone else."

She just kept looking at me and smiling, as if trying to see through my eyes. When I read in her book about the physical and mental abuse she was exposed to, it reaffirmed the greatness of her soul in my eyes, and she became like the most triumphant warrior to me. Titi has a tremendous desire for life; she is compassionate and love hovers over everything in her life—but more than anything, she understands the value of forgiveness. Today, Titi and I have a relationship that transcends words, a kinship that is hard to describe; it is a very deep connection that is sustained by absolute love; Titi taught me the true meaning of sisterhood.

Not to mention Laura, my oldest sister, my mentor in the entertainment world. One of my greatest desires as a child was to go watch her in the theater. I would work so hard in school to get good grades and to achieve the best possible report cards just so they would let me go see her. I loved being behind the scenes, seeing so many people watching her onstage, and she was always so calm, as if they didn't even exist—a consummate theater actress. I credit Laura with some of my first lessons: the way in which she would encourage me, to rid me of all my *ranchero* qualities, so that I could really face the public. My first appearance in a film happened because she took me to the set of *La Guerra de los Pasteles*, in which we both appeared in period costumes. It was Laura who took me on some of my first-ever auditions for commercials, and introduced me to her friend Paco Ayala, so that I ended up auditioning for the group that eventually became Din Din. I owe a lot to Laura for my artistic career, and for that I will be eternally grateful.

My two sisters, the oldest and the youngest second to me: I cried so much for them, and pleaded with God for them to come out unscathed. One of the images that most affected me was when Ernestina came home and, after spending some time with the family, decided to go out to the garden; she hugged a tree and began to whimper and cry. Trees carry ancient spirits and epic histories, and when one embraces them, they transmit a certain energy that anchors you to the earth once again. Ernestina's gesture of hugging that tree and crying with it showed her deep need to replant herself in the reality of her liberation.

The kidnapping did not end when my sisters came home, and it is really something that we will carry in our hearts forever; it is an event that tore my family apart. An ordeal of this magnitude causes internal damage in the structure of a family that endures such trauma, and everyone deals with it differently. While Titi and I remained extremely close—and we still are to this very day—the kidnapping wedged a painful distance between Laura and me, and for several years we stopped speaking. After everything she went through Laura felt that no one could understand her pain, and as much as I wanted to be there for her, there was nothing I could do or say to make her feel better. I could do nothing right. Molehills became mountains, and the distance between us grew wider and wider. It is difficult to pinpoint exactly what led us to such a negative and harmful situation, but the truth is that after the kidnapping we were all struggling with so many mixed feelings of anger, blame and resentment that perhaps we lost sight of what was most important: that we are a family and we are united by a bond of love. I wholeheartedly believe that time has a way of healing everything, and that God will one day return a sense of harmony to my family. Time is wise, and all we have to do is leave everything in the hands of God.

Up until my mother's death, we had so many mixed feelings and emotions. I am overcome with great nostalgia when I think about how much I loved the time that we shared as a clan, a matriarchy unified by a tremendous sense of love, solid and trusted, underscored by the monumental and mutual admiration that we all feel toward one another. When I think of how it took my mother's death for things to change, it hurts my heart, as if someone took a big bite out of it, and it cries out in these moments of such extreme pain. Of course, we share a sisterhood that will never, ever be erased, and between the five of us there somehow exists a solid sense of kinship that is utterly unbreakable.

Letting Go of Guilt

It has been a real challenge for me to release the feeling of guilt for the kidnapping of my sisters; it was months—if not years—of a lot of questioning and internal conflict. I felt that their kidnapping, and even the reality that they lived at the time, were all somehow my fault. My position as a public figure in Mexico and the fact that I am married to Tommy Mottola, a successful, powerful man, have made my family vulnerable to these kinds of situations, and even though I know, deep in my heart, that none of this is my fault, it pains me immensely to realize this. For such a long time I felt responsible for what happened; I kept thinking that if it hadn't been for me, my sisters would have never had to go through such a terrible ordeal. After a lot of introspection, along with the help of a therapist, I was able to understand that there is no point in thinking that way; I am who I am, and there is nothing I can do about it. Over time I have been able to recover my sense of security, my self-esteem and, most of all, to rediscover the meaning of forgiveness, starting with the forgiveness of myself.

Love is the energy that sustains everything, and it comes hand in hand with forgiveness. Among the many things that I did to release the tension, the pain and everything that I didn't like was employ a method used by many therapists and that, in my case, showed wonderful results. It involves writing down everything that hurts you, anything that makes you suffer, and to what degree you feel it. Then you fold the paper in half, tie it to a balloon and release it, saying, "I no longer want to feel this pain. . . . I am finished with it right now; I am going to be a free person, because I have everything inside myself to be happy. I have all the talents, virtues and everything that I have always dreamed of having. I acknowledge that I felt this great pain, this shame, and I accept it. To all the people who have caused me pain, I forgive them; it is time to release everything; it is time to let it all go." Thanks to this simple but powerful exercise, I have truly forgiven myself and rediscovered myself as happy and free.

This type of exercise can really go very deep, and should be directed by a professional, mostly because it forces you to accept yourself as you really are, to feel the pain in the deepest part of your being, to release it, to find the balance between suffering and liberation from pain, and to eventually be happy. And this is the exact path that I have chosen for the sake of healing the sanity of my soul from the most profound wounds of my heart.

Forgiveness has no memory, but we do. And that is exactly the problem. We should always keep in mind that the greatest teaching of Jesus Christ—who came to this world to suffer on our behalf, who was crucified and died for our sins—is forgiveness, and that we, through our sins, continue to crucify him. Jesus was able to forgive his traitors; he did not seek someone to blame; he didn't run to his Father to complain about what they had done to him. Even when they nailed him to the cross, he forgave, and, forgetting his own pain, he conveyed a message of hope and life: "Forgive them, for they know not what they do." His forgiveness opened the possibility of salvation, the path to truth and eternity. He is the path—the path to forgiveness.

As far as my sisters' kidnapping is concerned, I practically became my own flagellator; I carried the cross and crucified myself until I understood that I had to release all of that, because everything was already prescribed by God. It was part of my family's destiny, a body of water that the whole family had to get through and experience, in which we would all have the opportunity to grow and learn, without pointing fingers, without blaming anyone else. They are simply things that have been decreed since the beginning of time, which we have to survive, assimilate and face in the best way possible.

If you think about it intellectually, it is pretty simple to forgive with sincerity. But to achieve real results, during the process you have to first acknowledge that there is a problem, and you have to identify it. Second, you have to forgive yourself. Third, once you have accomplished the first two steps, it is important to forgive those around you. It is at that moment that it then becomes easier to understand that your suffering comes from the fact that you allowed yourself to be hurt—from participating in that suffering, from not knowing how to put a boundary on that suffering, for not learning the lesson on time, for judging or criticizing others, for whatever it is that's tormenting you. Acknowledge and accept your pain, and only then will you be able to forgive yourself and others.

Healing Wounds

Once my sisters were freed, Tommy and I suggested that they come live in the United States so that they could start to rebuild their lives. We did it in large part because the family of the kidnappers started going to Titi's house in Mexico and begging her not to testify against them now that the authorities had suspects in custody and were waiting for my sisters to identify them. With the situation so tense, we suggested that they move with their families, and guaranteed that we would help them find work and start a new life.

Titi accepted and sold everything she owned, including her house. She brought her daughters, and while they adjusted to being here, we helped them and supported them in everything they needed. We offered the same thing to Laura—for her to go to Miami, because she had friends there and could work for Telemundo or Univision, where they are always producing lots of soap operas. But Laura decided to stay in Mexico and, of course, we respected her decision.

When Titi and her daughters moved to New York, we found a very comfortable apartment in the center of the city, so that they wouldn't feel the change so abruptly, because in certain ways, Mexico City is a lot like Manhattan. They are both cities that never stop: lots of people, lots of hustle and bustle, lots to see, and lots to know. We wanted them to be as comfortable as possible, because coming here meant leaving everything behind—friends, status, careers, schools, stability and comfort—to come and try to explore something new. Even though we were helping them, that didn't mean that they were not leaving their whole lives behind in Mexico, the place in this world that they loved the most and knew the best.

Titi is a beautiful woman, blond and blue eyed, with a physique that is quite uncommon in Mexico. But in New York she was just another blonde; no one looked at her; no one knew who she was; nor did they care too much, and despite seeming like something insignificant, in reality it hit her very hard. Still, her pain required this space of total anonymity. She would walk through Central Park for hours. . . . She wrote poetry, and via therapy she began to write down her story, which ultimately became the manuscript for her book. It was very hard for her to be here, but thanks to the space that she was able to carve out in an unknown city, without even realizing it she began to heal her wounds. New York served as the perfect place for her catharsis, to release all the anger and helplessness that she carried inside because of the horror that she endured during those thirty-four days. And from coffeehouse to coffeehouse she started to write, and all I did was encourage her to do it. It took her about two years to write her book, because there was a lot of time in which she simply was not ready to remember the details of those days. When she started to feel secure again, be it in a Starbucks, at the park, in a little restaurant or in her own apartment, she became fully resolved to write. She also learned how to begin appreciating the city and enjoyed it as much as she could.

Four years later, at Rockefeller Center, where she worked as a consultant for Telemundo, she said to me one day, "Thali, I'm going back to Mexico. I don't want to be here anymore."

What? I thought to myself. *My sister is leaving me, my friend. . . . How can she be leaving?* My heart did not want to accept what my sister was telling me, but she just looked at me with those blue eyes, sweetly, the decision already made.

"Little sister, I'm drowning here," she said. "I need my Mexico, my people, my food, my friends. I love you, but I cannot live here; I don't belong in this place. It is very different to be alone on this path without someone by my side. Put yourself in my shoes and imagine yourself without your partner. . . . Would you stay here?"

I thought about it and realized that she was completely right. New York is a very tough city, and I am certain that if my husband were not a New Yorker, and if the majority of his business weren't here, I would undoubtedly be a Gypsy and wander elsewhere.

Titi missed her life, her friends and living among her people. She found it interesting that the men in Manhattan were ever pragmatic, without any desire for authentic intimacy, but with every urge to simply have a good time. My lovely Titi, such a romantic and in love with love, was not finding the man of her dreams, someone who would dedicate himself to court her by the book. She was used to the classic Mexican who sends flowers, opens the car door and falls in love first. The nostalgia began, and so she packed her bags and went back to Mexico—against my wishes, of course. She was scared to death of going back, but she would say, "I have to take a risk at some point, because I have learned to be myself; I finally faced myself, my dreams and fears, and I realized that a major piece of me stayed in Mexico." She always said that I had already fulfilled my dreams with my partner and my family, as I was already thinking of having my first child. But she had nobody, because her daughters were already grown up, and were starting to lead lives independently of her. That was how she went back, like a phoenix rising up from the ashes. That is how she left, and she continues to shine in Mexico.

I hate good-byes. And saying good-bye to my sister was very sad, but she was leaving happily, because she was also leaving with her book under her arm. She had released the nightmare from within and let it out in those 192 pages. Today she is the strongest woman in the world. I admit that I still miss her like crazy, because the truth is that we had such a great time here. We had a lot of fun, and it allowed me to have my family here; for me, it was the best, mostly because being together, and being able to help her start from scratch, allowed me to begin forgiving myself for what had happened. With her, with her help, and all the work that I did on myself, I finally understood that my sisters' kidnapping was not my fault. It was something that happened, that was destined to happen, and that was simply out of my control.

Meanwhile, Laura in Mexico released *Cautivas*. The play was very well received by the public, and filled the theater, which allowed the producers to extend the tour all over the Mexican Republic. Laura became very active in the war on kidnapping in Mexico, and she led various rallies for peace and nonviolence. Gradually, she also began to recover and recuperate from that traumatic event, and got back into her own professional life.

Life Lessons

Sometimes I feel that I have lived various lives, and that I have appeared on many different stages as I tread my path in this world. Artist, girl, adolescent, woman, actress, singer, daughter, sister, wife and now mother. How many faces have exchanged looks with mine? How many hands have I reached out to? How many dinners, lunches and events have I attended? How many stages have I stepped foot on? Words, events, people, moments— I think I have lived a lot, and at the same time I feel that my life is just starting and that I still have so much yet to live.

Taking responsibility for our actions is not easy, and today I know that before making any decision, I always assess the risk level; I analyze what the consequences of my actions will be. Maybe in one year I won't think that way anymore, because it is also true that as human beings, we are constantly changing.

Maybe in five years I would write something completely different on this page. But today, this realization gives me inner peace.

When we reflect and become conscious of our experiences, we can choose to be the victim, the tyrant, the judge, or we can take the fast lane of forgiveness. Ernestina could have opted to hate her captor every second of the day, which probably would have kept her far away from her present and her dreams. Still, she decided to release her feelings of pain, anger, helplessness, like a child releases a balloon and watches it disappear, never to see it again. In the end, Titi chose to walk on the path of forgiveness. In Laura's case the path was different, for she embraced faith with both hands, and every day she meets with her fellow believers to live it with all of her being. But regardless of the tools that they have chosen, each one has figured out a way to achieve tranquillity and inner peace in her life.

I have always been very realistic, and that means that I really like to analyze and revisit my heart to become better each day— more focused, sharing, open, willing to help those in need, whole—and, of course, to give space to my dreams and yearnings. I seek to have a clear vision of what my life is in the present, for me, for my family and for my friends.

With so many things going on in my life, sometimes I feel like an old lady . . . well, a very young old lady, youthful and happy. I have traveled a lot; I have seen so many things, but the trip that has actually taught me the most, the one that has given me the most satisfaction, has been the one that took me inside myself. During some very painful moments, during some other very intense ones, I have salvaged some invaluable riches from myself and discovered some unnoticed values in a great portion of my life. These values have allowed me to display more control and dominion over my person during certain moments.

Among the most unpleasant and painful moments that I have had to endure came when a Mexican tabloid magazine, without any sense of discretion, published photos of my father's ashes. Some degenerate journalist actually opened the urn holding my father's cremated remains and took photographs of them next to a little bag that held the remains of one of my grandfathers. The headline read: "Thalia Doesn't Take Care of Her Own Father's Ashes." Without any shame, they showed actual pieces of my relatives' bones.

The most painful part was to face the cruelty and the lack of humanity of these people, not to mention the lack of professional ethics, starting with the guards at the cathedral, the emblem of faith in Mexico, who allowed a reporter and photographer to remove the memorial stone, desecrate the remains of my father and grandfather, and obtain material with which to concoct a macabre article, which was then approved and published by the director of the magazine and his whole team, who sat around a conference table talking about how great it would be to feature it on the cover. I suppose the only reason they did it was to have more sales that week than their competitor, without any consideration for how much pain it would cause.

The photos traveled around the world quickly, and when we tried to find who was responsible, everyone played dumb. The caretaker of the funeral chapel where the church graves are located actually took a bribe and allowed this infringement upon the privacy of my family, but to this day, we still don't know who paid him. The cardinal never found out anything. The janitor didn't see anything. They all said nothing, so we never found out who the photographer was, or who had the unscrupulous mind to actually come up with this brilliant idea, so to make the blow even worse, we could not get to the bottom of it. We all know that when someone disturbs our dead, they are intruding on a spiritual plane that transcends what we are able to comprehend. It is a transgression against the most intimate and treasured objects that one holds.

Once again, forgiveness in this case was decisive. The motivating cause of the pain was different, but forgiveness is always the same: It repairs, it restores, but most of all, it liberates. It liberates you from reliving those feelings over and over again, placing you in a trance of anger; from a sensation that makes you feel a profound and uncontrollable sense of hate. When you forgive, it is as if you have forgotten about what happened. The most important thing is to remember that it is our choice to choose the path of forgiveness, instead of hate. It is in our hands to choose peace and tranquillity.

For my part, I choose forgiveness, because forgiveness is synonymous with freedom.

An undeniable truth is that you reap what you sow, and in great abundance, and ultimately all of us will have to take responsibility for our actions, thoughts and words. That is why I am so conscious of fixing all my mistakes here on earth; so that when I am no longer in this world, and the film of my life is shown, and I watch the scenes that I like the least, I will be able to say that I made mistakes but that I also knew how to ask for forgiveness.

I discovered a principal that is the primary axis of my daily life.

I discovered that love . . . is forgiveness.

CHAPTER SIX

Rebirth

D ear Sabrina:

My precious daughter, my beloved. As luminous as a little star, with ruby lips and honey-amber eyes . . . you arrived and turned everything on its head. With those little pearl-like teeth that always appear with your smile, I began to understand a whole new dimension of life. You brought new colors, new scents and new textures into my life. I rediscovered the world through your emotions, your words and your hands, those mischievous little paws, always investigating, discovering everything. From the day of your birth, you gave me a new sense of perspective that I had never known.

I am thankful for everything that I have lived; if I had not experienced the pain, the solitude, the sorrow and the greatest moments of darkness, I would have never known you.

*Now I understand the difference between night and
day; I fully comprehend the crack of dawn, when the
ascension of the majestic sun is announced to the universe,
when its rays of light, powerful and brilliant, disperse
the fog with the rebirth of each day. That sun, that
resplendence, lives inside of me, and with you, my
precious daughter, each day I awaken like a gladiator who
defeats even his most ferocious enemies. A new sense of
joy is born . . . my insides are reborn . . . and everything
around me is reborn. You have given me the ability to
resurge from the darkest parts of my being, to shine like
the sun, giving light and happiness to everything around
me. Rebirth at every instant, rebirth at every moment.
Rebirth. What a joy it is to have met you and to have you
in my life. As I walk with you, holding on to your hand,
every stumble, every problem, every pain transforms into a
precious gem that opens the treasure of life that you have
placed within me.*

*You know, Sabrina, what I most want for you is for you
to be able to be who you really are, unalterable forever. For
you to find that sense of respect for your person, your soul,
and never lose your own unique essence, knowing that by
virtue of nature's laws, it will happen at some point in
your life. But, my beautiful girl, the most important
thing—no matter what they say or think about you—is
that you always return to your essence and remain
authentic to yourself in the fullest expression of that
truth.*

*No one will love you more than you love yourself. No
one will respect you as much as you respect yourself. It all
depends on you. Perhaps you will buy into that distorted*

image of what it means to be happy, seeking it in people, situations or places. But at the end of the road, you will realize that satisfaction, sadness and melancholy all emanate from oneself, and that to find true happiness you don't need the biggest house, or the most lavish luxuries, and not even the partner of your dreams. All you need is to live in complete joy, to really understand your roots, from the deepest parts of your essence, and to dare to find balance between your virtues and your defects, your sorrows and your triumphs, your troubles and your greatnesses, you at your very rawest state.

Touch them, face them, assess them, know how to forgive them, and most of all, know how to strike a balance somewhere right in the middle.

Sabrina, when you know every nook and cranny of your essence, from your appearance to your emotions, from your heart to your intuition, you will become stronger and surer of yourself.

Be happy, my daughter. Be complete. Be ethereal and gentle with every step that you take. Be strong, yet subtle, like an honest tear. Be committed, but gracious in your character. Be open, but cautious, with the eyes of a lynx. Be audacious, but delicate like a rose. And most of all, my precious daughter, be free. Be completely free!

I adore you in every universe and on every plane that we exist, my love.

Rebirth

Not long ago, Sonia Hernández, the president of my fan club, MDC, reminded me of something that hadn't quite registered in my memory: "Do you remember the first interviews that you gave at the beginning of your career, when you talked so emphatically about your fears of being a mother?" she said. "And look at you now; you're already pregnant for the second time."

For so long, I feared that the things that caused anxiety would become a reality. The way my mind works, I could not stop thinking about the power of attraction, and I knew that if I continued to think about the fact that I wasn't able to get pregnant, I would only get farther away from my actual goal. When you focus on the negative, it is inevitably what you attract. My mind knew that it should stay focused on the positive, but in practice it was hard for me to execute.

Years passed, and I could not get pregnant. Treatments,

doctors, attempts and sorrows—everything happened before my Sabrina arrived. My insides were distraught and sad. I was missing something; I was missing being a mother, and I couldn't believe that I would be deprived of such a privilege.

One night in December, when I was talking with my sister Federica, I sadly asked her, "Why has God not blessed me with a child? Why do I have to go through this?"

"Little sister," she said, "you have to approach Him and spill your heart before His feet."

"But how?" I pleaded, practically yelling at her.

We spoke for a little while longer and later said a prayer together over the phone. I needed more from the presence of God; there were so many things inside my heart. I had asked for the forgiveness of so many people; I had come to a place of peace with everything and everyone. . . . But I had still not connected with the most important being of all: God.

After a powerful and beautiful prayer that penetrated the deepest part of my soul, Federica and I hung up and I continued my conversation with God. Suddenly the phone rang and I answered it, and it was her again.

"Little sister, God just showed me something amazing. . . . I had a vision of you at five months pregnant," she said proudly, and though I didn't understand what she was saying to me, her voice passed on all that enthusiasm to me.

"Sister, hopefully . . . hopefully God will listen to you."

"What do you mean, 'hopefully'?" she said briskly. "It is a fact. He showed it to me; a baby is definitely coming. Yuyo, God doesn't lie. It's true; you are going to have a baby." And she hung up full of joy.

By New Year's, she sent a gift with Titi: a green baby bag printed with little giraffes, which are my favorite. There were all kinds of baby items in that bag. I became so excited seeing this gift, but I put it away because I had already had my hopes up many times before, and each time the disenchantment always came with such great pain. So it remained locked away in my armoire, and I forgot about our conversation altogether. We continued to try everything, and nothing seemed to work. Gradually I could feel my hopes of becoming pregnant beginning to fade.

The Accident

We decided to take a vacation in Aspen, Colorado. I have always loved extreme sports and being adventurous, and when we go skiing, I always like to hit the "black diamond" slopes, which are the most dangerous. I like to do the riskiest things; in fact, it is a trait that I have always had: The sports I like most are skiing, mountain climbing and scuba diving in caves and cenotes, among other activites.

That morning I woke up with the desire to stay home. But shortly afterward, some friends called, inviting us to go skiing with them.

"Come on, get up," Tommy urged me. "Put on your ski clothes, and let's hit the slopes with our friends for a little while and we'll go eat lunch afterward." And after a bit of back-and-forth, I ended up sitting in the car packed like an onion, with three layers of thermal underwear, my ski clothes, a helmet in hand, gloves, boots, and my skis in the trunk.

Since I was a bit slow that morning, I had no problem drinking two Red Bulls, one after the other . . . incredibly dangerous! When I got onto the slopes I transformed into Speedy Gonzalez, or more like the Tasmanian Devil. Just like everyone, it took me longer to get back onto the slope than it did to ski down the mountain; I went so fast that the snowflakes themselves didn't even see me. After about twenty rounds, one after the next, and with a belly full of Red Bulls, I didn't realize how tired my legs actually were—my adrenaline just kept asking for more, more and more. Tommy and our friends were ready to have lunch, so I told them to go ahead, because I wanted to have one last run. But I lost sight of the fact that I was beyond exhausted. During that last run down, when I wanted my ski to make a turn, my legs didn't react, and I suffered a terrible fall. As I went down, I could hear my knee cracking. Seeing me fall so dramatically, the other skiers who were on their way down called the paramedics. Once I was rescued, I called Tommy and told him what had happened.

"My love, I fell. I am coming down on a stretcher. Wait for me down there; I think something is wrong with my knee."

Tommy, who had practically choked on his lunch, came to meet me and arrived just at the moment that I had one foot in the ambulance that was going to take me to the hospital.

I spent the whole afternoon in radiology, until the doctors diagnosed a fissure in my tibia, along with a few torn ligaments. The result: total immobility of my leg, splints, ice bags, crutches and lots of rest. I was advised to rest at home with my leg up, and most of all, no New Year's party. I had to take it easy, and with these instructions I went home.

I took it all with as much good humor as I could, adorned my crutches with Christmas bows and bells, and made the best of the situation. Maybe I needed to rest, and the accident was the only thing that would make me listen to God, because it stopped me in my tracks. It didn't take me long to realize that, as with everything in life, there was a purpose to what had happened to me. I became so relaxed that I even managed to stop worrying about the pregnancy, about work, about the trips. . . . All I did was relax for a couple of months, watching a marathon of Mexican movies starring Jorge Negrete, Dolores del Río, Pedro Infante, Tin Tan, Joaquín Pardavé, María Félix and Mauricio Garcés, all while sitting still in my house. That's when I fully understood the meaning of the expression, "A watched pot never boils," or the other one that says, "If you love something set it free; if it comes back it was always yours—if it doesn't, it was never yours to begin with." Because there are moments when a human being clings to a love, or insists on going after a certain job, or goes out of his way to make something happen—but the more he struggles with it, the farther away it puts him from his dream. There is a wonderful saying in English, "Let go and let God," which pretty much says it all.

The Surprise

I started to feel nauseous; I wouldn't eat and I thought I had anemia, so I went to the doctor, who gave me a full blood panel. We were home when we got the call with the results. "It's important that you come to the office; I have something to tell you," he said to us. That is not the kind of call that one expects, much less for the doctor to tell you that he wants to see you in his office. We got very nervous. Once we were sitting in front of the doctor, Tommy and I grabbed each other's hands, expecting the worst.

"Okay, here goes . . ." he began. My mind was hit with a barrage of questions: *What is it? Is it something serious? What has he found?* But the doctor interrupted my thoughts. "Are you ready?"

What anticipation! I just wanted him to let it out already; the silence was so overwhelming. Finally he let it all out at once:

"You are going to be parents. You have a baby on the way."

Tommy and I screamed. *"What?"* We looked into each other's eyes, which filled with tears, the news penetrating both of us in the deepest part of our beings, and we were completely overwhelmed with joy. We felt as though someone had just informed us of a miracle.

The doctor recommended that I get a lot of rest, something that has always been a challenge for me, because I don't know how to sit still. Even so, I took my pregnancy very seriously. Just thinking about the chance that my baby would not make it to full term mortified me, so I would lie in bed and prop my legs against the wall or drape them over large pillows, and I'd grab a book to just relax.

As the months passed by, something began to happen inside me. Just as my body started to change, my inner being was also starting to change; I didn't recognize myself. I felt that motherhood was going to be the most exciting adventure of my life. *God is so wise,* I would think to myself. *If I had not gone through everything that I did, I would never enjoy this moment as I am enjoying it now.* I had been forced to take a break from my crazy career, and now I had time to go into a state of introspection, to clean my house, or my inner temple, my mind, my soul and my body, shake off the dust, and to remove things from the experiential and emotional drawers that no longer served me. Someone special was coming into my life, someone who should not have to face the chaos that came with me.

We kept the pregancy a secret for the first three months. Not even my mother knew. We were so afraid that something might happen and that we would be faced with explaining something as painful as the loss of a baby—not something that I wanted to endure. But the day came when I told my mother, and she couldn't believe it. She was so overcome that she ran around with her arms up in the air as a testament to her jubilation, crying, "My daughter . . . my little daughter!" The hardest thing for both of us was to keep the secret from my sisters. My mother had always been my best friend, and I knew that she would carry a secret to the grave. But the poor thing had to work to hide her excitement from the rest of the family, especially because everyone was saying that her daughter Thalita was acting "mysterious and quiet." Taking advantage of the long distance, we were able to hide it until I was five months pregnant. Granted, you could see the news in her eyes every time she and I exchanged glances; we were like two little girls keeping a great big secret, signaling each other with our eyes not to run off and tell the whole world.

I got to my fifth month and called Titi to invite her to spend a weekend at our house. The first day she didn't even notice. The second day we went out to lunch, and when we came back to my house she came to the bathroom with me, and I lifted up my shirt to uncover my belly. I said, "Look at what a belly I have! I think I might have eaten too much, sister."

"Actually, yes, you do look a little bloated." I gazed at her with a smirk on my face until she said, "Are you pregnant, Thali?" and she started to cry so hard that the tears seemed to shoot straight out of her eyes.

We hugged for a very long time and started jumping up and down together. We looked like a couple of crazy women! I had to tell her to stop shaking me because I was in a fragile state. She immediately called my nieces, and I called my other sisters. When I reached Federica, she said, "What's up, little sister? How are you?"

Trying to control my voice, I said, "I'm good. I'm calling because I have to tell you something—"

And before I could continue, she burst out, "You're pregnant, right? How many months along?"

"How do you know?" I asked. "I haven't told anyone . . . but I'm five months pregnant."

"But of course!" she yelled exuberantly. "Remember when we talked about God back in December? After we said the prayer, He showed me a vision of you five months pregnant. I kept asking Him when that would be, because so much time had passed since the moment that He showed it to me . . . but of course! You were at five months in that vision, and right now you are at five months. What He was trying to say was that you would tell me of your pregnancy at five months."

My sister was so happy that she didn't stop talking. Of course . . . God had already announced it to us.

Once the rest of my family heard the news we gave ¡Hola! magazine the exclusive, as I thought it would be the best way to share it with my fans. After my sisters' kidnapping and the wounds that were healing in my family, I avoided the press for a very long time; I needed to give myself some space away from everything that happened. But I definitely wanted to share this piece of news with the rest of the world.

I took such good care of myself throughout my entire pregnancy: I practiced prenatal yoga; I did light weight training; I walked; I read everything on how to prepare for motherhood; I ate healthy, macrobiotic food; I drank no alcohol; I meditated and did breathing exercises.

When I was in my eighth month, I began to feel very tired. My mother was with me during the last few months of my pregnancy, and when I would tell her how I felt, her answer was natural. "Oh, honey, it's normal; a baby takes everything it can from its mother: her calcium, her vitamins, everything. . . . It's consuming you, honey. It has to grow big and strong, so it is totally normal that you feel this way. Rest and sleep as much as you can, because afterward you won't have time for any of it."

I had a feeling it was going to be a girl. The first time Tommy and I talked about having kids, we agreed that we wanted the first one to be a girl. It is amazing how much a person can change. Before, all I thought about was my career and my albums, and now my thoughts were completely focused on my baby. I could not stop thinking: What would she look like? Who would she look like? And what about her personality? I would try to imagine whether she would be sweet, serious, smiley. . . . I was consumed with curiosity—and, of course, with the selection of a name, which would be such a crucial part of her identity. From the beginning, I wanted something like Gina Sabrina, or just Sabrina. We liked the name a lot because it sounded very Italian and carried a certain kind of strength. And when they confirmed the baby's sex we practically went nuts. In one of the many baby-name books my friends gave me, I found the name Sakäe; we liked how it sounded next to the name Sabrina, and besides that, it meant "prosperity" in Japanese. Sabrina means "princess," which meant that we would have a princess of prosperity in our house. "How beautiful," we said on the day that we chose her name. "A little queen of prosperity is coming into our lives!"

The Birth

My water never broke, but the contractions began on October fifth at around one in the afternoon. At first I thought it was the typical cramps that come at the end stages of pregnancy, because according to our calculations, the doctor's and mine, I still had a few days left. But the contractions kept intensifying, and with

them the pain. By midnight I started feeling more regular contractions, and the pain was a clear indication that the moment had
arrived. I waited as long as I could, but at around four in the
morning I said to Tommy, "We're going into the city, *now!*"

We live on the outskirts of New York, and it usually takes us
about forty-five minutes to get to Manhattan, which is where my
hospital was located. So we thought it would be a good idea to go to
our apartment in the city and wait there until the morning. But by
the crack of dawn, we were already with the doctor examining me.

"Thalia," he said, smiling, "you're only dilated to two centimeters."

"What do you mean, two centimeters—that's it?" I was a bit
confused, because I was expecting to stay in the hospital and deliver the baby. Seeing his expression of "you still have a good
twelve hours," I thought to myself: *What is this guy smiling about?
Of course, since he's not feeling what I'm feeling, it's easy for him to
send me back home. . . .* And that's just what he suggested, that I
go home and come back around six in the evening. So we left.

Since I knew that I would not be able to withstand that pain
for a whole day, I called our doula, which is someone who spe-
cializes in caring for women during birth. During the last month
of my term, she had helped me a lot, giving me special preparatory
massages, and now she and Tommy calmed my nerves, my anxiety
and my desire to go running out of there. But by five o'clock, I
couldn't take it anymore. I could not find a comfortable position
that would alleviate the contractions—not standing, sitting, lying
on my side, squatting, in a warm bath, sitting under running
water, receiving massages on the lower back—and nothing,
nothing could take away the pain. I couldn't even breathe. Everything irritated me, including the very robe that I wore; I was cold,
I was hot, I cried, I laughed, I sweated, I took off my slippers and

put them back on. . . . *Help! Somebody help me!* I was desperate. In my mind, visions of women from ancient times appeared, those who gave birth at home, or went outside to hold on to a tree branch as they squatted down and delivered a baby just like that. What courage! In that moment, all I could think about was how they could do it. . . . *What do I grab on to? Give me a branch!* They were true heroines!

Anyone who has gone through labor knows that there are moments when you lose all sense of composure, etiquette and good judgment. A part of you starts to emerge in response to the unrest, desperation and unsettledness that come with regular contractions. For example, at one point I called Rosita, an amazing woman who has worked in my house for many years—actually, I screamed to her: "Rosaaaaaaaaaa!"

Rosa came running and asked, "What happened, love?"

With another scream, louder than the first one, I said, "Tell the fucking car to come right now, and tell Tommy to come now or he will stay here . . . and if not, he can go to hell . . . but I am going to the hospital now!" Poor Rosita had to endure all my rudeness. I already apologized to her, but I will do it again publicly: I am so sorry, Rosita!

Tommy had insisted that I wait as long as I possibly could, because I would be more comfortable at home. Of course, he was right, but only those who have experienced contractions can understand my desperation. Besides, in times of crisis, the foulmouth in me comes out; María *del barrio* appears, and no one can stop me. It is very liberating when one feels desperate; I don't know why, but it's always worked wonders for me! When I was a little girl and was acting hyper, my mother would take me to the parks or to Chapultepec, and she would say, "Honey, run all over the field and scream out your favorite curse word with every last bit of air in your lungs," and I would run around like a mad child, screaming, "Ass! Ass! Assssss!" Half an hour later I would come back to the car, periodically muttering, "Ass . . . ass . . . ass," in whispers now. The strategy worked.

As we drove to the hospital, Tommy didn't stop talking: "Baby, take it easy. We're almost there. I love you. . . . Baby, we are one minute away. Calm down."

You calm down! I thought to myself. With my face glued to the car window, I breathed through every contraction, completely drenched in sweat, with the windows all fogged up, desperately waiting to see the entrance to the hospital. As each contraction began I felt a wave of heat all over my body, and I had to think about relaxing so that the pain would not be so intense. After each contraction, incredible heat would travel all the way up to my head, all at once. You know those cramps in your legs and lower back, which are multiplying, and without asking your permission, break into the tug-of-war that's going on between your pelvis, coccyx and lower back . . . never mind the lateral pains that make you feel like there is something wrong with your kidneys . . . and your husband sitting next to you saying, "Baby, I love you . . ."? All I could think was, *Where do I hang him?*

When I finally arrived at the hospital, a doctor offered to give me an epidural to relieve the pain. I don't know what was worse—the thirty-centimeter needle in my vertebrae or the contractions themselves. The injection seemed to take an eternity, and in that moment, all I wanted to do was kick him. The anesthesiologist was a bald man, about forty years old, with something of a pit-bull gaze. When the medicine started to take effect it was amazing, and so great was my relief that I patted his bald head, gave him a kiss and said ardently, "I love you! You have no idea how much I love you!" Tommy and the nurses were dying of laughter. But I was serious.

The problem was that I would not dilate and the hours kept passing. When my doctor arrived, he examined me and said, "You haven't dilated at all. You are still at two and a half centimeters, and if you don't dilate within the next two hours, we'll have to do a C-section."

"A knife to my body? No . . . Doctor, please don't make me have a C-section; anything else, but not a C-section!" I said, pleading with my eyes.

He said that he would have to do some manual stimulation to open my uterus. He told me that it was like squeezing an orange and that it could be done only three times, and carried a risk of infection that could be fatal. The only other option was to do a C-section. I screamed at him, "So squeeze the *fucking* orange already!"

After thirty-two hours of labor, the real struggle for my baby to come out began. It took me an hour and ten minutes before the magnificent head of my beautiful daughter began to emerge. The little miss had a big old head—heady in every sense of the word, my baby. She was born at three in the morning.

One month earlier I'd given the doctor a list of requests, which included my request for a mirror positioned where I could see her come out, and told him that the moment she came out, I wanted her placed right on my chest so that I could have immediate contact, with her skin against mine. I also wanted to cut the umbilical cord myself. The doctor said, "Are you crazy? I have never allowed a woman to do this." But I threatened to switch doctors, and he ultimately agreed.

There in the delivery room, with my baby on my chest and my husband by my side, the doctor saw the magnitude of our bliss. He said, "The moment has come to cut the cord. Thalia . . . are you ready?"

I exchanged glances with Tommy and said, "Yes." So I grabbed the scissors and told Tommy to put his hand on top of mine, and we cut the cord together. What an amazing moment—what a flash of eternity. I ask God only that when the time comes for my daughter to assert her independence, her father and I will show the same courage in cutting the emotional and sentimental cord, so that she can be a free woman, forever supported by us.

When I saw her face and those little eyes searching for mine, and her tiny little hands, I kissed her and I began to cry. It had all been worth it, all that pain, those thirty-two hours of struggle, everything, just to see her, and we were finally together. "I adore you, my love; I adore you," I kept telling her. We were both crying uncontrollably; in fact, I think Tommy was the one who cried the most.

When they were giving me the epidural, I told him to go to the bar where we'd first met and have a couple of martinis—one for me and one for himself—to call our close friends, and to start celebrating. In fact, his only job was to film the action. When he came back, even feeling the effect of the martinis, he took the best shots and the best footage that I have ever seen. Spielberg and Scorsese have nothing on him! I would have given him an Oscar. With a camera in hand, he filmed me all the way to the delivery room; he captured the moment our baby came into the world; he filmed our faces crying from joy; he was euphoric as he interviewed everyone around.

Today that recording is a precious testament of a yearning that God has realized in our lives, a yearning that came full of smiles, joys and life. All cleaned and ready, Sabrina was placed in my arms, but I immediately took off her swaddle blanket so that I could see the sheer perfection of God in full display right on my bed. As I swaddled her again, I talked to her nonstop: "My princess of prosperity . . . we are finally together; I can at last hold you in my arms, my beautiful little one. My Sabrinita . . . my Saky . . . my daughter."

While I was in the delivery room, my dear friend Anne Glew had come into my recovery room and decorated everything in pink. She had brought pink sheets, a pink comforter, pink pajamas, pink towels, pink trash cans, and even the shower curtain of the bathroom was now pink, a pink toothbrush, a pink soap dish, everything pink. My entire room was pink and smelled new, just like my baby—she smelled like a certain kind of newness, something that I had never sensed before.

Sabrina

With the birth of my daughter I felt that until that day I had been nothing more than a spoiled little girl. Of course, now I am only a spoiled woman, so it's not that the dynamic has changed all that much! It's true that I love to be pampered by my husband, my fans and my sisters. Only now, with more consciousness and the maturity that came with the arrival of Sabrina, I know that I have a responsibility to raise a human being who will one day stretch her wings to fly in search of her own destiny.

When Sabrina came into my house I turned into a spokesperson for antibacterial wash. Tommy had to look at the positive side of my obsession, this renewed compulsion against germs. "Baby, if you want, we can launch a line of your own sanitizer, and we can call it 'Thaliatizer,'" he would say, laughing at his own joke. "Or we can invest in Purell. What do you say? It could be a good business." It was just that my baby seemed so vulnerable that I was petrified of something happening to her.

As Sabrina continued to grow, I discovered that she was a lot like me—for example, in her delight over food. Every so often we escape to eat some meringue-filled cakes, and chocolate and va-nilla ice cream, which are her favorite. We go on these dates alone, just the two of us, against her father's will—he would rather see her eat tofu and vegetables all day. I agree that she should eat in a balanced way, but it is also true that I am a Mexican, and I love to eat my traditional candies, my ice pops made of sweetened condensed milk, my wafers and, of course, my Garibaldis, which are little pancakes with jam on the outside and little white bits of sugar called *chochitos* on the inside. Whenever my mother came to see us she would bring us Garibaldis. My daughter would wait impatiently for days until her grandmother arrived with her breads filled with white *chochitos*. Since I let her eat only one per day, she savored it like nothing else; if one little *chochito* were to fall, she would find it with her finger and it went straight into her mouth. She wouldn't waste a single crumb.

To care for, forge and educate a child is a tremendous respon-sibility. It is true that being a mother is a job that never ends. One day, when I was still pregnant, a woman asked, "When are you being 'cured'?"

"What do you mean, when am I being cured?" It was a question that I didn't understand. I was pregnant, not ill.

She answered, "Pregnancy is an illness that lasts nine months and a convalescence that lasts for an entire lifetime."

And in a way, she was right, because you really do dedicate a whole lifetime to your children; your children continue to be your babies even when they themselves are parents.

Being a Mother

I cannot stop thinking about all those mothers who work, some-times two or three jobs at a time, even with all the responsibility of taking care of their children, and besides that cook, do laundry and iron—women who help their partners like equals, or who face the world alone to make sure their children turn out well. Women who are a part of the history of humanity, who one way or another ensure that their families prevail. Brava, I say. They are so courageous. I deeply admire them.

Only when you are a mother do you begin to understand certain things about your own mother. I had the opportunity to speak with her extensively about the daughter-mother relationship, and sometimes I would ask her, "How did you manage with so many daughters? I have enough to do with just one! How did you do it?" Because back then women had lots of kids, and they were nurses, cooks, cleaners, educators, teachers, doctors, psychologists and friends—they were mothers.

My mother was born in La Paz, Baja California, a coastal village that was then an open port where everything came in from Asia. My grandmother, whose name was Eva, decided to take her and go to live in the capital. Only twenty-six years old, with an ironclad character, a woman who would stop at nothing, she left her land for the first time. They had it rough for a very long time, because they had absolutely nothing or no one in the capital; I don't doubt for a moment that my mother was the real Marimar, a little coastal girl who suffered tribulations from birth, from the time that she arrived in the capital until she was married and, awakening from the nightmare, ultimately became the great woman that she was known to be.

Now I understand all the things that my mother had to endure with my sisters and with me. Somehow, with the options and the tools she had at the time, we turned out to be good women, women who love life, who enjoy simple things like a smile, a sunset, a rainy afternoon, but who at the same time are warriors and winners, who fight for their ideals. When or how she did it is a true mystery to me. But what I do know is that I want to take those aspects of greatness from my mother and, as a mother myself, transmit them fully to my own kids.

I have learned that in this life there is no one to blame, that there are only victims of victimhood, that the patterns of life often repeat themselves from generation to generation. Today I know that all I can control is the ability to retain or to release, and I discovered that it is ultimately more satisfying to release. Whatever is truly yours will remain, and whatever doesn't never was.

Like me, Sabrina lives in two different worlds, anchored in two different generations: Her father grew up listening to Frank Sinatra, and her mother, Guns N' Roses. We are from two totally different generations but have joined together to become mutually enriched. I believe that the result is going to be fantastic. . . . It was with me. I am the consequence of a great amalgam of eras, tastes, predilections and ideas that were present in my family, and I am happy with the way I turned out, with what I am and who I am.

My household is growing, because even as I write these lines I am awaiting the birth of my second child. Sabrina will have someone to play with; she will be the big sister, the teacher, the one who already knows the path. She will be the great hurricane that forms from the abundant Mexican culture and the intense Italian culture, from the two typical flavors of my country, from the social gatherings innate to Italian-American families, from the echoes and sounds of our motherlands, from our pasts, from our history; she is part of the new generation, but enhanced by the richness of our traditions, and with these tools I have no doubt that she will always be my princess of prosperity.

CHAPTER SEVEN

FAITH

$\sim$

Beloved Father, glorious Lord:

There is no one like You, who loves unconditionally.

I know in the deepest part of my being that You plucked me from my mother's womb, where I was taken care of until the day You came knocking on the door to my heart; and when I stood before You, as You waited for me to invite You in, it was the most perfect and glorious moment that I have ever experienced in my life.

Thank You for loving me; thank You for forgiving me; thank You for one day telling me that I was like the apple of Your eye; thank You for treating me like a daughter. Thank You for everything You have given me, everything that I have understood and also that which I have not. Thank You, because even when I don't like the way something turns out, I do understand that everything has a purpose. Thank You for teaching me the value of life.

Thank You for taking me by the hand and guiding me from the darkness into the light. Thank You for all the tests and difficult moments that You made me endure, because You are forging me and making me like tempered steel; I am in the process of becoming a soldier who goes from one victory to the next.

I am only one more on the path, passing by like a hiker, following the trail that You mark along the way. I ask only that You do not allow me to detour and that You give me the wisdom to build my house upon solid rock.

Thank You for being my Father. . . . Thank You for desiring me in Your heart, and for reaching out Your arms to embrace and carry me.

With all of my being, and everything that I am, I hope to one day come before You and to run into Your arms, saying, "Abba . . . I tried. Father of mine, I'm home."

Faith

Faith . . . A tiny word that contains such massive significance. It is not something that you can buy in any way; faith comes when you hear a certain truth, and truth can be a special person . . . the special person of God.

I understand that there are various interpretations of God's magnitude, which is why He is omniscient, omnipotent and omnipresent; He can be found in a sunset, in the stars, in the eyes of a child, or in any other representative element that comes close to the divine. For many, God dwells in a small porcelain statue, or in saying novenas with rosary beads in their hands; these are figures and gestures that make a person feel closer to God. To me, God is the energy that consumes everything, that breathes in and out like a fire or a force that emanates from all your pores, your atoms, and that you clearly know lives in everything, every one of us. God is not limited, like a person; He goes beyond what our minds are able to comprehend; there is no one word that can explain it, but you feel it—you live it.

One day while I was reading the Bible, I found a verse in the Gospel of John that remains etched into my heart. Jesus prays to God "that all of them may be one, Father, just as You are in me and I am in You" (John 17:21). A certain clarity opened up my comprehension and I understood: We are one, which is why I am You and You are me. This phrase turned into my mantra: "I am You and You are me." I said it over and over again when I became sick, and it sustained me and gave me the necessary strength to battle Lyme disease.

God in My Heart

I have always considered myself a spiritual person. Ever since I can remember, God was spoken about with respect in my home. The figure of God was always present in my house, and like so many other children, I learned through repetition; I memorized all the prayers to give thanks, to go to sleep, to eat; I went to Mass on Sundays, during Easter, and on Ash Wednesdays. But having someone tell you is not the same thing as feeling His presence in your very own heart. For many years, my relationship with God was not very different from that of most people. His name was always on the tip of my tongue, and my connection to Him mostly consisted of my asking for things, even mundane favors—from help passing a test at school to my mother not finding out about my mischief—until the day finally arrived when I felt His presence so authentically that it shattered all my preconceived notions that I ever held about Him. On two occasions in my life, God came before me, allowing me to see Him in all His glory and grandeur.

The first time was in the early nineties, when several members of my family were gathered in my sister Gabi's living room, and we started to say a prayer. Through Gabi, salvation graced our family; she was the first one who had a spiritual encounter with God. Later on, He gradually came knocking on all our doors.

That afternoon, we began to sing some praises to God, and afterward each one of us said a prayer, one by one. My eyes were closed, and in some kind of vision, I suddenly saw that Jesus was present. With my eyes still closed, I could see Him walk up to each one of us and stand before us. My heart started to race uncontrollably, a sense of joy flooded my whole body, and all of a sudden, He was in front of me. From the other side of the room, my mother said, "He wants your heart, Thali." I saw Jesus bring together His precious hands, but when He stretched them toward me, I instinctively closed my shoulders and crossed my arms over my chest in a gesture of self-protection. But Gabi, who was sitting opposite my mother, gave me some encouragement: "Give it to Him. . . . Give Him your heart. . . . Let His light enter you." I could not understand how two people located at opposite ends of a room, with such different perspectives, could see what I was seeing. How could they know if all our eyes were closed? I saw it as a confirmation that it really was Jesus who was standing before me. So I lowered my arms and saw Him take my heart and then place it back in, installing a beam of resplendent light inside my chest, returning to me a new and radiant heart.

When I felt that powerful light enter my body, I started to cry from happiness, and for the first and only time, my lips began to sing a harmonious melody that I didn't know. The voice that came out of my throat was not my own; it was more like a trill, an angelic sound, almost baroque or medieval, a beautiful voice. It was a spiritual chant that allowed me to sing perfectly on just that one occasion. I lost sense of time, temperature, of who was around me. . . . I even lost sight of the fact that I was standing in a physical place. God had touched my soul; He had exchanged a heart of stone for one of flesh. That day I began to understand eternity. I understood that God is a real being, that He is real and always by my side.

My second encounter with God's love came a few years later, in the mid-nineties. It was a Sunday morning. Some family members and I were at Gabi's house again, all of us dressed in white, because we were going to become consciously baptized, unlike when you are a baby and it is your parents who make the decision. The house was all set up for that moment, and there were many people standing around the circular pool singing praises unto God, waiting for our turn to go in. When it was my turn, many things passed through my mind, but the moment my pastor submerged my head beneath the water, everything stood still: I could see underwater, so I contemplated the open skies above, God on His throne, the many angels present in the atmosphere, and I understood the meaning of the expression "A great celebration is held for the remorse of just one sinner. . . ." In that moment, the sinner was me, a rueful sinner who came out of the water feeling free, unlocked from her chains, frustrations, pains, sorrows, sadness, everything—anything that was no longer relevant to me, so that I truly could become free, full and complete.

After these powerful encounters, I went through a few years of feeling a deep need to better know God through His word, to better understand my life and my daily experiences, as I saw them all projected in the biblical verses. Many of the psalms became my protective shields, and from the beginning to the end of each day I felt happy, finding strength through prayers, music and praise.

Over the years, my relationship with God stopped being as intense as it was when I first encountered Him, but no matter how busy I am or how hectic my life may become, I always make it a point to reconnect with that ever-living presence that was awakened in me. I am able to keep Him present in my daily life through prayer, that direct dialogue that we all have with Him, and as often as possible I get together with my prayer group to recite. I have always needed the presence and protection of God, for myself and for my loved ones, and He has been a presence throughout the entire trajectory of my life. The day I saw the magnificence of God in the moon and asked Him to bring me close to love, the day that Tommy and I prayed together in our wedding chapel, or the moment when He showed my sister Federica my pregnancy . . . all those were moments in which I was drawn to His presence. In all the various stages of my life, during the most important moments, He has always been with me.

I think about how many moments in our life He has been with us, just as He said: "I will be with you on all the days of your life, until the end of the world," and I believe it. There is no question about His promise.

The Mystery of My Illness

I was eight months pregnant when I started to feel physically sick. I didn't know what was happening to me, but I had turned into a very sedentary person because I was always exhausted. Everyone said that it was because it was my first baby, that it was normal, which was why I didn't worry too much. But once Sabrina was born, things didn't really improve. I went from feeling bad to . . . much worse. "You have postpartum depression," my primary doctor would say. "It's going to pass." "It was a very long labor," the gynecologist would say. "Don't worry." Even though they focused on depression because of how bad I felt, I knew with wholehearted certainty that I was not depressed or sad. Nothing could have been farther from the truth. I was really ill, and we simply didn't know it.

The doctors even ended up prescribing antidepressants, which I never took. I kept saying, "You're wrong; this is the happiest time of my life." Finally, after so many years of struggle, I had my daughter in my arms. This was not postpartum depression! But they didn't care what I said. It was as if I were talking to a wall. They didn't hear, or it was more like they didn't want to really take my opinion into consideration. Later on they would say that it was the breast-feeding that was draining all my energy. It was true that I didn't produce a lot of milk, but why would that drain my energy? I didn't buy that explanation. Then they changed their minds and said that it was a hormonal problem, and that maybe it was because my thyroid was reverting back to the way it was before my pregnancy. Other doctors disagreed and said it was anemia. . . . There was no way to get them to agree; everyone had an opinion, but no one knew for sure, which unleashed a terrible frustration and rage in me, which I had to deal with on top of how bad I already felt.

The main symptom was my total loss of energy. The exhaustion would worsen every single day, and I started to notice that my muscle mass was beginning to diminish, too. I was consumed by such an extreme fatigue that just the simple act of thinking would leave me monumentally tired. It became so severe that I couldn't even hold my own baby.

"Father," I prayed, "please give me the strength to breast-feed my baby; please give me the strength to get out of bed to take care of her, because she needs me strong and healthy." I made the effort to follow all the instructions that the experts gave me . . . but nothing worked. I continued to feel like I had been run over by a truck that had dragged me for a thousand miles, along with a steamroller that had crushed every last bone in my body. I literally felt that I was dying.

The muscle pains were terrible. There were moments when my body would not respond for me to even get out of bed. There were other times when I would just cry and cry, saying to myself, *How is it possible that I cannot even hold my baby in my arms? How can it be?* These thoughts would barrage me over and over again, while I tried to move forward.

Around five months after I gave birth, while we were in Florida, I woke up one morning and smelled the proximity of death. The "bony one" was in my presence; I could even see it in my peripheral vision. But unlike *La Llorona*, the lost soul who wandered and lived in my childhood home, this presence—dense and heavy—was actually death itself: icy, sharp and ready to grab me by the hand and take me with it, never again to return. I got out of bed with great effort and stood in front of my husband. The certainty that I was leaving was so real that I said, "Tommy, look at me, and enjoy it as much as you can, because I am dying and I feel like this is my last day." Tommy, of course, became extremely alarmed, and we went right back to New York, where we began to work with an entirely new fleet of doctors, studies, hospitals, analyses and all kinds of tests. Three months of my life passed like that, and still nothing.

I would spend the whole day in bed resting. But every time I had any energy, I would search the Internet for illnesses that seemed relevant to my symptoms. After hours and hours of reading and research on every possible medical Web page imaginable, I discovered that the conditions that most closely resembled mine were lupus and Lyme disease. I was determined to find out whether I had one of these conditions, because if not, I could at least discard them as possibilities—but the symptoms were very similar to each other. So I asked my primary-care doctor to please test me for lupus and Lyme disease. I already knew that there were only two research labs that specialized in the detection of Lyme disease, with more accurate results than anywhere else, one called IGeneX in Palo Alto, California, and the other one in Stony Brook, Long Island. Shortly after my blood tests were sent to these labs, the result of the research confirmed my suspicions.

"Thalia," the doctor said when we went to see him to obtain the results, "I have good news and bad news. The good news is that you're right: You do have Lyme disease. The bad news is that you're in a very delicate situation, as the illness has advanced."

Because of the tone of his voice I could feel my stomach shrinking in fear of the unknown. I squeezed Tommy's hand so hard that he could see the bones in my hands.

Lyme disease is an infectious disease caused by the bacteria *Borrelia burgdorferi* that is transmitted through ticks. And that is exactly what happened to me—a tick bit me and gave me the Lyme bacteria. The illness is also known as the "great imitator," because its symptoms are so general, it can be confused with chronic fatigue, dementia, blindness, depression, fibromyalgia, multiple sclerosis, lupus or Alzheimer's disease, a fact of which I am living proof. It is a silent sickness, capable of deceiving the body in such a way that doctors are often unable to diagnose it. If not detected in time it can become chronic, which requires that the patient take very potent and aggressive antibiotics for years, possibly for life. When the tick bites, it often leaves a round, reddish mark, which is known as a "bull's-eye," and this is the optimal moment to attack the disease with antibiotics, to prevent it from spreading into the rest of the body.

After the bite, the sufferer may experience coldlike symptoms such as fatigue, body aches and headaches, dizziness and nausea, as well as other symptoms that affect the central nervous system and cause a hypersensitivity to light, radical mood swings, anxiety and insomnia. In some cases, it affects the facial nerves, which can lead to facial paralysis.

There are four stages of Lyme: primary, secondary, tertiary and chronic, depending on how long it takes doctors to diagnose it. In my case, I never saw the tick or the bull's-eye—nothing. It was almost a whole year after I started showing some of the first symptoms that the disease was finally detected, and by then I was already in the chronic phase. This meant that the bacteria had spread through my whole body and infected all my organs, including my heart, brain and, more than anything, my central nervous system.

As my doctors explained it to me, the danger of this illness, which at first glance doesn't seem so terrible, is that it attacks your central nervous system, which can cause irreparable and irreversible vascular damage. Many patients are left paralyzed, others blind, and some even lose their ability to speak. In the worst cases, it costs them their lives.

I had to deeply know my illness to understand what was happening to me, and with this information I created a Web site, www.sobrelyme.com. It is my goal to raise awareness, as it is a disease that is not taken as seriously as it should be, mostly because of the lack of information about the subject—even in the very laboratories and medical fields where it is being diagnosed.

When you're in the chronic phase, as I was, the infection becomes resistant to any type of antibiotic. This complicated everything. As we attempted to stop the disease in every way possible, I became overrun with medicines. The toxicity was so severe that I experienced another condition called the Herxheimer response, in which a medication intensifies one's symptoms. Sometimes this condition is confused with an allergic reaction to the medication, but it actually stems from the toxins released by bacteria as they're killed by the antibiotic. All of the flulike symptoms and shivering are really part of the body's process of ridding itself of the toxicity. So I not only had Lyme, but my body was also reacting negatively to the medicines I was given to treat it. As they say, when it rains, it pours.

I spent months lying in bed, feeling as if I were dying, and with very little desire to live. I felt that it wasn't worth it to go on living like this. I related to all those people who suffer with terminal diseases such as cancer, who are subjected to chemotherapy with side effects so aggressive that they sometimes have moments when they feel it is hard to keep on fighting.

Thank God Tommy was always by my side. I can attest that he fulfilled his marriage vows with all his heart, "in happiness and sadness; in sickness and in health," because he was right by my side all the way through. Sometimes he had to carry me to the bathtub, where he would place me in the warm water, wash my hair and comb out the tangles while I cried and cried and told him to leave me alone, that I couldn't take it anymore.

"I don't have the energy to keep on fighting. . . . Please, Tommy . . . just let me go. . . ."

Choking on his own sobs, he would say, "No, baby, don't say such silly things. You're going to get better. Sabrina and I need you. You're going to get better."

He was my nurse, my caretaker and my companion. He dressed me, he put my pajamas on, and he fixed my hair. I was a total skeleton, and he never showed me any expression of rejection, of alarm, of anything. He would often say tenderly, "You look beautiful, my love. Put this color on; you're going to look gorgeous; it's going to cheer you up." He would get me into the car and drive me around; he would take me to see the sunsets; never, at any moment, did he allow me to fall.

The biggest problem was that the medication was making my symptoms worse, but I could not stop taking them. It was terrible! I would sweat profusely, soaking my pajamas, the sheets and even the mattress; everything hurt, even my hair, which, by the way, started to fall out. At times it felt as if my head were going to burst, as if there were lead inside of it; my eyes ached in their sockets, and sometimes it felt as if there were metal marbles buried deep inside my head. All of it amounted to nights of insomnia that totally precluded any rest. My joints would pulse as if my heart were beating inside each of them. It felt like someone had pushed a knife straight into the joints and was trying to detach them; it was excruciating pain. The hypersensitivity of my skin was so severe that sometimes I couldn't even handle the bed-sheets. It felt as if a hot chili had been rubbed all over my skin, or as if the skin itself were being removed. And the muscles . . . what muscles? I no longer had any strength. I had thinned down to a skeleton of about one hundred pounds. Whatever was left of my muscles felt as if they had been flattened with a steamroller. My central nervous system made me feel cramps, flashes of electricity that shot through my whole body. My hips and legs felt as if they were joined by a metal beam that I couldn't move, and my hands lay open constantly, because I didn't have the energy to close them, much less to hold on to anything. Every time I wanted to walk, it seemed unlikely that I could even stand, and I had the sensation of boiling water shooting down into the soles of my feet, as if I had walked on hot volcanic coals for hours.

When the Lyme infection is very advanced, another symptom that appears is memory loss. One day when my sister Titi was visiting, she tried to chat with me to cheer me up, and I remember looking at her and thinking, *I love this woman; I know she is my sister, but . . . what's her name?* I even got to the point that I couldn't communicate and couldn't even form sentences. I lost the capacity to mentally organize, to plan; I was in some kind of vegetative state, like I was there but I wasn't. . . . Vegetating . . . Floating . . . Outside of reality.

I was on antibiotics for two years, including five of the most potent ones. I was injected with penicillin every other day, the treatments lasting for so long that there was no space left on my gluteus for more injections. My butt looked like a sack of little marbles: balls everywhere that were already hardening because the medication had made contact with the tissue. I was also given a medicine that attacks malaria, and many other injections that I had to take daily to strengthen my immune system. I was taking all of these drugs with the sole purpose of killing the bacteria, but they were really small doses of poison that not only attacked the infection, but in the process also started to kill me. Between the injections, the pills, the nutritional supplements, vitamins and herbs, in total I was taking about fifty pills per day. It was horrible.

Defeating Death

There were days when I was not even conscious of time, and among them many days when I had no will to live. One of those days I was lying on my side in bed, the very place where I had spent so many months, when suddenly I started to feel a certain sensation in my body. I immediately thought it was that moment that I had read about in several books, the moment of leaving your body, of dying, of letting go and flying. . . . I felt that this was my moment. *If I want to go,* I said to myself, *I can go.* It was such a comfortable feeling, so completely pleasant, without the sensation of any pain, like total liberation, a certain heat that made me feel that I belonged to everything, that I could transcend, leave everything and be free. . . . It was very powerful, and in that moment I decided that I would go.

The baby monitor that let me see and hear my little girl from her crib was on, and just then she started to cry, a terrible wail out of the blue, as if something were happening to her, a cry that seemed to shatter the atmosphere, a cry that brought me back. I immediately returned to myself. I pushed back the sheets of my bed, stood up and, grabbing on to whatever I could, I made my way to her bedroom. Standing in front of her crib—and I don't know where I got the strength, since for weeks I had been too weak to lift her—I picked her up and could finally hold her close to my chest.

I walked over to an armchair in some confusion, because my baby was no longer crying. She was simply looking at me, emanating such peace and love that I was totally consumed. I saw myself in her eyes, and allowed myself to be caressed by her beautiful little gaze. I asked myself how it could be possible that just a moment ago I had made such an overwhelming and egotistical decision without thinking about her, about this tiny defenseless creature who totally relied on me. "Little one," I said, "I will do it for you. I will fight on. No matter what needs to happen, I will battle in this war against death, and I promise you that I will come out of this." I closed my eyes and said a prayer: "Lord, give me the strength I am lacking. Please . . . hold me. I am You and You are me." And I sat there with my little one in my arms, talking to God.

That was the day I decided not to submit to death. Seeing myself in the palm of God's hand and kept warm by my own unbreakable faith, I could finally sleep as I had not slept in months, because I knew that the battle was already won.

My mother didn't leave my side the whole time, never stopped supporting me, holding my hand and giving me faith. She spent all those months worried sick, and that same night, seeing me with my eyes closed, she still felt the fear that she might never again see them open. Taking advantage of the fact that I was finally resting, she went home to change clothes, and sometime later she told me that on the way to her house—which was about fifteen minutes away from ours—she started to cry. She was so afraid of losing me. When she got to her bedroom she began to scream and raise her voice in desperation. "Father!" she screamed with all the pain that she carried in her soul, "my daughter is dying; my daughter is dying. . . . I don't know if she will wake up. Please help me, because she's dying!"

Desperate, between sobs, and with the heart of a mother who knows her daughter is dying, she grabbed a Bible and opened it to a random page, as if she were looking for a sign from God. Her eyes landed on a passage that described the death of a nobleman's daughter, when Jesus sat at the foot of the bed and said, "*Talitha kum!* Little girl, I say to you, get up!*" In that moment, my mother felt a great peace in her heart, and she knew right away that I would be saved. For her that verse was particularly affecting because she affectionately called me Thalita. So she took a shower and lay down in her bed with the certainty that her prayers had been heard and, even more, answered. Whenever she saw any of those symptoms that sent me back to bed, her faith was so immense that she would say, "*Talitha kum!*" with certainty that I would get up.

From the day I heard my daughter's cry in that moment of such absolute desperation, my mind changed completely. I honestly don't know how it happened, if it was in my thoughts, in my conscience or in my attitude—but slowly I underwent a change that allowed me to move forward. Three years after I began to feel sick, and after almost two years of extreme treatments, the doctors finally got the disease under control. That does not mean it totally disappeared; it simply means that I will remain in remission as long as I take care of myself and respect the changes that I needed to make for the good of my body.

Today I am on the road to recovery. Since I began to feel better, I made a new goal for myself: to get to an optimal state of health, with my symptoms under control. My health became my number one priority. Today there are trace amounts of bacteria in my body, and I am fully enjoying the benefits of the goal that I imposed upon myself. As with every goal, I had to put in a lot of effort and work hard to reach it, which has resulted in a change of lifestyle, nutrition, exercise, and optimism, and in focusing my thoughts on the simplest things in life. I have learned how to release stress and the moments and situations and things that make me anxious. That last one is very important, because stress lowers one's defenses, it debilitates the nervous system, and, in my case, it allows the bacteria to more effectively take over the body. My life today is dedicated to zero stress, zero negative thinking, excellent nutrition abundant with fruits, vegetables, nuts, seeds, juices, proteins, and a series of natural supplements, and constantly keeping my body in motion. I know that this is part of my therapy, and just as diabetes causes a person to change his or her lifestyle, Lyme's disease also changes your life forever. If I eat sugars, breads, pastas, or very greasy food, or drink alcohol, I know I will have two weeks of symptoms to look forward to and require a whole detoxifying process to eliminate everything that I ate. Today I meticulously think about whether I want to give my body that kind of jolt, because my body immediately reacts by making me go through many horrendous days as the toxins are all expunged.

Today I know that I am the only one responsible for my health; it is in my hands, and I am its guardian, its caretaker and its fiercest defender. But the most important thing, even more than my health, even more than my mind, is the knowledge that I am in the hands of God, because with every step that I take in my life, He nourishes me and fills me with strength, reminding me that I am a warrior, and that if I walk while holding His hand, this battle is won.

The Trapeze

When I think about those terrible years that I lay in bed without being able to move, I am consumed with images of sadness, pain and confinement. They are the very images that fill me with energy, reinvigorating me, along with an insatiable desire to experience everything. In this search for new experiences, one day during the summer of 2010, with my health back to about ninety percent, I decided to get on a trapeze. I have always been very flexible, and with yoga, my body still retains a lot of that flexibility. After I had recovered from Lyme disease, my muscles were left totally flaccid, and they required extensive toning. As a child I always wanted to be an Olympic gymnast, and after seeing Nadia Comaneci win her gold medals in 1976 with a perfect ten, I yearned to be just like her. After beating the worst parts of the disease, I looked for a way to make that a reality and to grant that wish to my inner child.

One day when I was driving down a road in the Hamptons I saw a huge sign that said, TRAPEZE LESSONS HERE. So I got out of the car to get more information. I immediately enrolled, and a few days later I eagerly arrived for my first class. Everything was new and exciting, all the more when I looked at it through the experience of having beaten death and recovered all of my ability to enjoy everything around me. I began my ascent up a little ladder, which didn't seem too steady, and my heart started to race like crazy. On the platform about nine meters up they put the harness on me, and it occurred to me that I was about to launch myself into a massive void. Despite the fact that they had all kinds of security measures, including a mattress below in case someone slipped, I felt my heart drop. I compare it to the same kind of tension I feel when I am about to go out onstage to perform; it is like a rash of heat that starts in the feet and travels up to the belly, where it forms a knot. Your mouth dries, your body freezes, while a powerful force begins to come up from within. The moment you hit the stage, that energy explodes and transforms into freedom and emotion. That terror that you feel turns into the certainty that you can overcome the situation with the best parts of yourself.

When I was up there, with my hands on the trapeze, the instructor told me to bend my knees and lean my torso forward before jumping. So I visualized what she was saying, took a deep breath and went for it, without fear. I swung from one side to the other, unstoppable; I went up and did it again countless times, as many times as I could. That very first day I ended up daring to jump into the arms of the instructor, who hung from the other trapeze. I liked it so much that, champion obsessive that I am, when I finished the lesson that day, I was "almost" ready for Cirque du Soleil.

I liked that feeling of freedom so much, it completely filled me; I found a recreational exercise that allows me to stay fit, mentally and emotionally. The trapeze has allowed me to understand five truths that I always try to apply to my life. First, have confidence in the instructors and their security measures. In much the same way, God is my instructor, and everything that I endure has security measures that were designed by Him. Second, you have to be willing to climb that scary little ladder of the trapeze to get to the top. Even when my situation seems very precarious and unstable, like that ladder, I have to go on and defeat all fears, every obstacle, to see my problem in its proper perspective. Third, it is crucial to quiet all negative thoughts, the ones that say, *What the hell are you doing all the way up here? You are a mother and shouldn't risk your life this way,* and exchange them for, *You are so strong and brave when you put yourself up to the task.* You have to release all disorderly thinking into the hands of God, and allow Him to impose His victorious thinking and a life lived fully. Fourth, it is important to release your fears, anxieties and limited attitude and make the leap, knowing that the arms of God will always be there to catch you. And fifth, enjoy the journey and live it intensely, and every time you are about to jump, it should feel like the last time you are going to do it. And the truth is, when we live such intense moments in the face of pain, doubt, lack of understanding, death, it is important to know that God is there with His immense love, His strength and His great light that envelops us with protection, happiness, joy and life.

One of the most important life lessons that I acquired over the last few years, and especially after my struggle against Lyme disease, is that you have to dare to live life intensely, giving yourself up to the present, to the moment, fully enjoying the experience before you, exploring, investigating, inventing, imagining, dreaming, being an unlimited being. It is crucial to think beyond the mind's parameters, to be audacious, and most of all, to have joy! Life passes way too fast to waste it on sorrows; you must not forget that everything has a solution . . . except for death.

That's why you have to live life to the fullest!

CHAPTER EIGHT

CONCLUSION

D

ear Future:

You always live in the present, a time and place where you don't belong. But there you are, a part of every single one of my plans, my projects and my deepest desires.

You blend in with the present in such a natural manner, and you don't care whether you come in the shape of my dreams and desires. You focus my thoughts with such intensity that you become the organizer of events, gatherings, parties, vacations, studies, appointments and meetings, preparing it all very quickly and with extraordinary care.

Together we've dreamed big; we've imagined magical moments filled with splendor—and the most astonishing part is that you have kept your word. How many times have our plans or goals materialized before my eyes? From the little girl who dreamed of one day getting married in

*Saint Patrick's Cathedral in New York to the teenager
who, locked in her room with her eyes closed, imagined
stadiums filled with people singing her songs and
screaming her name. Today I understand how important it
is to hold your hand and visualize my dreams. I realize
that when I do, giving it all my heart and soul, the world
conspires to give me what I am looking for. It would be
hard to explain to others what you and I come up with in
our own private meetings.*

*Future, you will never cease to be by my side; you are a
fundamental part of what is yet to come. I have had the
opportunity to reflect on this relationship, and I have
decided that you will continue to walk with me in my
immediate life plans and my great dreams for what lies
ahead.*

*I ventured dangerously close to death, and at that point,
dear Future, you almost disappeared. But now that I have
returned as a strong and complete woman, I realize that
your company made me lose sight of many precious
moments of my present.*

*I discovered, dear Future, that my happiness walks
hand in hand with the present.*

In the process of writing this book I discovered so many things about myself that were hidden in some dark and dusty corner of my soul. I realized how wonderful it is to be alive and to live life with intensity, passion, adventure and a desire to win at everything. I realized that at so many points in my life I was afraid, terrified of being myself, of respecting my values, my beliefs, my founding principles, and as a result I had to go through some difficult moments, some very unhappy periods. But today I can look back and realize that if things hadn't unfolded exactly as they did, I would never have been capable of facing life with courage, like a pirate with his face to the wind, navigating through the turbulent waters of my emotions and feelings, conquering unknown lands in search of the treasures that are hidden inside me.

A Product of My History

The effort and courage it has taken me to sit down and evaluate my life offered me a real perspective on my present and has brought about balance and a self-confidence that has allowed me to value the person I am today. I understand now that I am a being in a constant state of change, and that what matters most is that I am able to identify my lowest or most difficult points so that I can avoid falling into that quicksand where I am unable to turn my life around, in search of a freer and more secure path where I feel a hundred percent myself.

I have discovered that if I apply what I have learned over the course of my existence, I have a better chance of attaining positive results. Human beings are the product of their history, their past, their roots; therefore, by understanding my weaknesses I am able to make myself stronger. Even though it's true that I have to live my life in the present, it's also true that I must project myself toward the future that I will necessarily build or destroy. The many life lessons I have learned along the way have given me the mechanisms that allow me to face any type of situation, as long as I accept my past responsibility and recognize my part, even in the cases where I am not proud of what I have done, without blaming anyone else. It is important to see myself the way I am, admitting my mistakes. I believe that is the first step toward true sanity and self-acceptance.

Every phase of my life has taught me so many lessons. I've learned through hard times and extremely painful experiences as well as moments of great tenderness, beauty and love. After all, that's what life is about: a never-ending spectrum of emotions that we need to experience, face, conquer and live through. With every passing year, these lessons have allowed me to find the value in what I have experienced during each phase of my life.

Childhood is, no doubt, the time when the basis of what we will eventually become is set. I was able to discover this as a child when I came face-to-face with silence and death, two realities that were a strong part of my life during those years. I gathered all my strength until I was able to break the silence that had taken over my soul after my father's death. A child's mind and heart are so fragile, and the person who perceives a child's pain and takes his hand in order to help him out of it is very special and important. My mother and my sisters were key figures in my path to recovery, and I am grateful that I was surrounded by so much love and warmth at a time of such a devastating tragedy.

Sadly, not all children are lucky enough to have that sort of support when they are growing up. In my travels through so many countries and my encounters with so many people, I have come to realize that children can also become the perfect victims in the hands of abusive adults who weigh them down with their own powerlessness, restlessness, anger, rage and countless other emotions that they are unable to channel in a better way. So many children have been hurt, emotionally poisoned, rendered incapable of developing their abilities and their gifts, their personalities weakened, limited, humiliated, despised, abused. . . . The list is long and the harm is often irreparable.

However, it's also true that children come equipped with extremely potent weapons, such as forgiveness, the ability to forget, loyalty and unconditional love. Over the years, children can come to lose these powerful tools; sometimes they even forget about them completely. However, I have managed to reconnect with my childhood, and I give myself every opportunity to learn from everything I experienced when I was a little girl, and I never cease to reflect on the innocence of those years.

I was able to express this feeling in a song called "*En Silencio*"

("In Silence"), which reflects on everything I was going through back then. Both my childhood and my youth come together in the chords of this song that explores the need to resonate with others. Once a person finds what she wants to fight for, a new song beats in her heart, making her feel like she can fly without limits, sing without limits, live without limits, even while deep down inside she can remember the silence that once wrapped her entire soul.

I've learned to listen to and understand that little girl who lives inside me, and now I give her the space to do many of the things I wasn't able to do when I was young. I've understood that there is no one to blame—there are only victims of other victims—but I also learned that only I have the power to change how the present will define and impact my future.

The Girl Within

My first step in the process of reconnecting with my soul and finding the anchor I was lacking in my life was daring to face my childhood. I needed to give myself a chance to talk about my most intimate childhood fears, doubts and pains. I had to embrace that little girl who lives inside me and assure her that those sad and difficult days are gone and they will never come back. I've learned that I have to make sure that I always give her the best, and I must also allow myself, from time to time, to be that child who just wants to run, play, have fun and most of all to love and feel accepted. It is only then that I was able to begin to know myself in order to walk down the path of forgiveness, security and fulfillment, to rescue and restore myself.

But as I embarked on the path to reconnect with my childhood, I faced the temptations of a globalized society, where power, glory and fame are more important than our own internal values and needs.

Human beings usually seek success in order to be recognized and respected by others, in order to achieve a status that's higher than others', and in doing so, they sacrifice many vital things that should never be forgotten. I wasn't responsible for determining my professional life; it evolved naturally, but ever since I was a little girl I've worked hard to do my job in the best way possible. In this whirlwind of experiences and lessons learned in the great school of life, I connected with worlds I didn't even know existed. Sometimes these worlds caused me much pain and loneliness, as well as an arrogance that prevented me from seeing my own mistakes, a huge ego, and a type of self-confidence that was far from the much-needed confidence in my inner being. I will never cease to be grateful for the many experiences I have lived and continue to live. Thanks to them, I was able to recognize that something was missing, that I wasn't a complete woman. I had many shortcomings, and there were voids that I was incapable of filling, that I was able only to patch, depending on the moment. The truth was I didn't know what was going on; I didn't even understand myself. I wanted one thing and then another, but in the end I was always in the same place: alone, unable to understand what was happening to me, and with a strong desire to run away. Sometimes it's necessary to fall and take a whack! You have to "break your teeth," as we say in my country. If I hadn't fallen as hard as I could fall, there would have been no possibility of restoring myself, no possibility of freedom. It was the only way to start healing my soul. It wasn't until I reached the lowest of the low that I realized I had two options: I could either embrace denial and blame whoever was around for my present condition, or I could confront myself and take charge of my life.

My Life in My Own Hands

By taking responsibility for myself and accepting my place in the world, I was finally able to truly find myself and walk a new path. This was when I began to recover.

In fact, taking responsibility for myself meant getting back on the track that I was always meant to be on, that is, becoming a whole and complete person. It's by taking responsibility for myself that I was able to say no to suffering, self-punishment and self-pity. That is the true meaning of glory.

It has been important for me to attempt every one of my conscious, positive and correct actions. Doing so allows me to see the fruits of the successes I have reaped for not falling back on what I have learned over the years, on what I inherited from my family, my society, my religion, and therefore betting everything I have on choosing to renew, rebuild, rescue and give myself the opportunity to start over. It hasn't been easy, but it isn't impossible. By trying, I was able to taste the glory—not the glory of money or social position or a relationship or a work project—the glory that comes from feeling fulfilled by who I am, from being sought out for who I am and not what I have. The glory that comes from being listened to with respect, when my words are taken as life wisdom. That, for me, is true glory; that is success; that is freedom.

How many times have we used the word *freedom* without understanding its true meaning? Throughout history the word *freedom* has been used in opposition to the idea of slavery, captivity, subjugation, oppression, tyranny and abuse. How many families have at their core one or several of these attributes? How many families suffer the tyranny and abuse of one member who has subjugated the rest of the family? At what point did cowardice take over the heart of the man who is unable to fight or defend his "personal territory"? How many people have grown up under these circumstances and reproduced the same behavior as they grow older?

God created us with the freedom to choose. Our free will is what has become enslaved in so many ways. How many times do we do what others expect of us simply because of our desire to feel accepted? How many people fail to defend their ideals for fear of being ridiculed? How many people lead a gray existence because they are unable to stand up for their thoughts, ideologies and beliefs? At what point did we lose sight of eternal and divine freedom? I don't know, but I do know we can get it back. I also know that one can defend one's ideals, even when the process is painful or uncomfortable, even when it involves ridicule or contempt. I've lived through it myself, and I know that it can be done, and that freedom is one of the biggest treasures I have gained in my journey throughout this world. I was able to free myself from codependency with my mother, from my fear of independence. I was able to break free from my obsessions and my phobias, from the frantic pace of my work life—a veil that wouldn't allow me to enjoy life. I was able to leave my country in order to become an immigrant, someone who is from neither here nor there, even though I will always carry the eagle of my Mexican flag wherever I go. Through these struggles I was able to find the space to rethink my life and, like a lamp amid total darkness, that introspection led me toward the light of freedom.

Breaking Free

Freedom—or liberty—should not be confused with libertinism, because in the end, the latter is a death trap that leads you to fall prey to outside circumstances. When it comes to being a complete individual, freedom does not hurt anyone. By discovering this wealth of wisdom, I learned to respect the ideas of others. I learned that if someone doesn't agree with me, it doesn't mean that they are wrong; it simply confirms that each and every one of us is unique in our own way. Freedom allows me to know myself at my best, as well as the potential that lies within me. Today I fully understand what Benito Juárez (former president of Mexico) meant when he said, "Respect for the rights of others is peace." By respecting the ideals of our neighbors without sneering, belittling or boycotting them, we will learn the true meaning of peace and the freedom to express ourselves without harming others.

We are responsible for finding the path to freedom that we all yearn for. In this search there is no one more important than ourselves. If we do not love ourselves, we will be incapable of love; if we do not respect ourselves, we will be incapable of respecting others; if we are not free, it is because we have not allowed others to be free. It's a difficult task, but after all, the best things in life are hard to get.

With freedom, I finally found the path to love. The most important love is the love for ourselves, because we will never be able to love another person if we do not love ourselves first. By strengthening this backbone of love and self-esteem, I was able to make my life as bright as the sun, to radiate well-being, love and joy to all those around me, illuminating my days and enriching my relationships. That love can even reach those who are here without being here, such as my father, my mother and the Rebel, right along with those who are still here with me, such as my sisters, my husband, my friends and all those who have at some point played a part in my life. Likewise, love extends itself to those who have hurt me, who have set traps in my way or who have wished me ill. By merely imagining these people wrapped in a blanket of love and well-being, I can offset the negative feelings that they have sent my way. Love is something you cannot see but you can feel. It's like air: You can't see it but you can notice it on your face; you can feel it in your hair; sometimes you can even hear it as it whistles by . . . but what's most important is that without air you would not be able to live. Love is the core of life. It exists beyond the mind. It means giving without expecting anything in return. It's the wheel of happiness and joy. It's wishing that someone else be happy even at the expense of one's own happiness. Who can love always and unconditionally? The only example I know is God Himself, whose love for us was such that He gave us His son for our salvation.

But His divine essence is in every pore of my being. That essence is what allows me to continue on toward a goal, a desire, in a specific direction. I know that for love I do things that might seem crazy but are in fact ways of giving, showing and offering what I am made of.

True Love

In the same way we must give and share love, we must in turn be receptive and open, without expectations, in order to receive what love has to offer us. In fact, most of the time we fall short in what we expect from love, because once we find it we are surprised by its perfection and intensity.

When I longed to find the love of my life, in my heart I already knew that I wanted him even though I didn't know him yet. Very deep inside me I knew that the person I wanted to share my life with existed. When I had him before me, when I got to know him, when I lived with him, I realized that love is not a solid feeling that appears embodied in one particular human being. It's more like a flowing energy that transforms itself, and in order to keep it we must work to take care of it.

No one ever taught me how to keep the flame of passion alive, but my longing and the fervent desire I had for my love to be permanent, not just a passing sentiment, allowed me to start working on building our life together. That meant maintaining a balance among acceptance, tolerance, desire, support, friendship, intimacy, respect and, most of all, commitment. All these elements are essential to a strong, secure and durable love. It's a daily job; every day I build my home with a smile, a caress, a kind gesture, a word of support, a little gift like a flower, a note, a message . . . anything that will allow me to remain close to my loving husband.

Yes, it's hard! Often you have to give in and please the other person, but you will always reap what you sow. If you sow scarcely, you will reap scarcely; if you sow generously, you will reap generously. You must plant these seeds in the hearts of your friends, your coworkers, the person you love, anyone you interact with in your home, at your workplace, at school or in any other environment. This is how, every day and for all these years, I have learned marvelous lessons on coexistence, tolerance and acceptance.

In addition to the family I was born into, I also have the blessing of the family I chose. How can I not be happy? The harmony that reigns in my home is the result of much work that is crowned by something that cannot be bought or stolen . . . *love*.

But just as life is capable of giving us the wonderful gift of love, that all-encompassing power, it also has the ability to deliver moments of extreme darkness. Moments when you are at the very bottom, and you discover your deepest essence, your rawest reality. When events one day fall upon me and crush me when I least expect it, that's when my truest self emerges; circumstances are out of my control, and there is nothing I can do to stop the rush of emotions, feelings, thoughts, attitudes, actions and words that come up from my depths. These events are often what are most painful for a human being, like a fight, a robbery, a death, an accident or, in our case, a kidnapping. These are things that forever scar your soul. There is a saying—"What doesn't kill you makes you stronger"—and that is exactly what an experience like this can do to you: It can annihilate you or it can help you find that powerful force that each and every human being has inside. It's a force that allows you to get back up, evaluate what happened and overcome it. But you have to uncover it. Instead of asking myself, "Why did this happen?" I ask myself, "What did this happen for? What is the lesson I'm supposed to learn? How can I use it to grow stronger?"

The Power of Forgiveness

One of the most beautiful gifts that I treasure, especially at times when I don't understand why certain things happen to me, is forgiveness, without a doubt. Without forgiveness there is nothing. Nothing else helps me move the heavy burden that hangs over my soul when the unexpected immobilizes me, affecting my surroundings and putting a halt to my time and my life.

I've had to learn to be brave to forgive. I know that I will be able to forgive only if I have a sincere and noble heart; I have learned that in life only forgiveness can restore, strengthen and heal the soul. It is hard to forgive. One has to struggle with so many thoughts and feelings. That is how my personal struggles unfold, the struggles that devastate and depress me, leading me to a state of disarray in which sometimes I cannot even get out of bed in the morning. But when I am immersed in that dark sea of internal conflicts it's so beautiful to finally see the light—it is the light that offers salvation, security and life, and when I grab on to it, I can embark on the path to victory. I recognize that I am weak, but that the things I cannot handle don't make me fragile. Instead, they give me an unsuspected strength that will help me rise to fight a great battle for myself, and I discover that I am rewarded when I give it the last blow with the weapon of forgiveness. And in order to forgive those around me, the first thing I need to do is forgive myself.

It is impossible to recover the past; I cannot go back and undo what I have done or said. What I can do is start today, and the first step for me has been to stop being my own executioner, my most severe judge. I've begun by forgiving myself, and from this moment on, I have created my own basis for acceptance and understanding. I've learned to stop tripping myself up and start on a new path waiting to be discovered.

Forgiveness has brought about understanding, freedom and the restoration of my being. Step by step I have discovered what forgiveness holds for me, how it can offer me the opportunity to be reborn, to open up to new horizons and great ideas that can bring me a fresh and original life concept. The idea that being born, growing up, having children and dying are not all it's about. There is more to life than just those things.

A New Life

After so many experiences and moments often painful and difficult to assimilate and accept, I have had no choice but to reinvent myself, recover and be reborn. As many times as necessary, I have looked—and continue to look—for ways to renovate my life, because every conflict I face, every struggle that does not kill me, allows me to recover and be reborn with new expectations, new goals and new objectives.

One of the times an inner force drove me to continue when I did not want to go on was when I had so much trouble getting pregnant. Trying again and again, the pain of believing that we had finally conceived, and then the disappointment of discovering that we hadn't . . . those who have been through such an experience can understand that my heart was devastated, crying and silently screaming, begging to have the child I so deeply desired. I had to endure many years of painful searching, until one day I was finally heard and I got my little girl. Joy took over my entire being, her presence completing our family bliss.

Not a single day has gone by without my learning something from my daughter. With her I have rediscovered the world. I see it through her eyes as I peek into the world of childhood, a world that already seemed so far away, and at times I allow my inner child to play with her. I have discovered aspects of myself I did not even know existed; for example, I've started to write stories based on my daughter's life in order to help her understand why, at her young age, she needs to experience certain difficult moments, such as saying good-bye to her pacifier! I never cease to wonder at how she accepts these realities with great courage, if not without the occasional tear, of course! Children are so beautiful; they have such a clear and transparent way of seeing life. I often ask myself, When did I stop seeing it that way? As I grew older, my existence became more complicated. I'm not sure whether losing this sense of clarity is a defense mechanism or if it's because I didn't want to have to explain my actions. The truth is that I replaced simplicity with complexity without realizing that in fact all I was doing was wasting my time. When I removed the invisible chains that I started carrying along the way, I could enjoy wonderful moments, take pleasure in common, everyday things, such as a ray of sun, a singing bird, a flower growing through a sidewalk crack, a rainbow after the rain—so many beautiful things that cross our paths—and realize that I am alive and that each day gives me the opportunity to start anew and be reborn into a life of love and freedom.

After the incredible experience of giving birth to my daughter, life threw me the challenge of having to endure a long illness in which I saw my body weaken, my muscles deteriorate and my face reflect the features of a long and painful ordeal. It was not easy. There were times when I was poised between life and death, and times I refused to take the fifty medications I had been prescribed, including two years of daily penicillin injections. There was no longer a spot on my body to inject the needle, and I wasn't even able to stand on my own two feet. As my body deteriorated day after day I went into such a depression that all I wanted to do was sleep forever. It was a feeling of indescribable sadness and despair.

Coming out of this state has been one of the biggest challenges of my life. Only with the love of God and the support of my friends, fans and family, little by little, was I able to recover.

The Power of Faith

Ever since I was little I have heard people talk about faith, but the truth is, I didn't know how to get it, how to embrace it in order to claw my way out of the difficult state I found myself in. Who could assure me that I would no longer feel the pain that invaded my eyes, my brain, my joints, my arms and my legs until my hair hurt, let alone the pain I was feeling in my soul? But divine wisdom always has its purpose, and when I heard my baby cry and was able to make my way to her room, when I saw her and understood that she deserved to have a mom filled with life and strength, I decided to do everything I could to get out of the state I was in. I learned that life is filled with decisions, and that day I made a decision for her and for me: I had to recover. I had to learn to control the pain until I could stop feeling it. I had to work hard to rehabilitate my limbs, which were emaciated and sore. I began to climb back up the hill. It was hard; it was grueling, but not impossible. Day by day, week by week, month by month, my condition began to improve. The doctors saw my efforts, which were bearing fruit. As I got stronger they started to remove drugs from the list until I'd practically quit them all.

Today, almost four years after that day in my daughter's room, I can assure you that if you have faith—faith in whatever it is you want to do with your life, even when you can't see the immediate results—you can achieve whatever lies in your heart. As I write these pages I am nearing the last months of my second pregnancy, and by the time this book comes out and you have it in your hands, I will be holding my little one in my arms.

Moving Forward

For me, one of the most important things in life has been to learn to make decisions and put them in motion without taking my eyes off the goal. If we do not set things in motion and take action to face life with security and confidence, no one else will do it for us. Taking action is essential in the essence that moves me through life, so that it doesn't remain stagnant. Nothing is impossible when we act and we have faith, for faith can move mountains! And from the top of the mountain I can catch a glimpse of the flash that, like dawn, marks the arrival of the future that will crystallize my dreams.

Talking about the future is always uncertain, because, in fact, we are projecting something that has not come, something intangible. Of course, the future is in my projects, my goals; it's a vision and a mission that needs to be shaped and built in order to obtain the hoped-for results. But regardless of whether that future is near or far, the fact is I can live it only in my mind and my imagination, and if I cling to it too tightly I may lose the precious gift of living in my present, my here and my now.

When one of my biggest projects, my live album *Primera Fila*, became a reality, I wanted it to be about my most personal self, my life experiences, my deepest essence. For the first time I wanted to show my audience who I am today, without regard to whether the album would be successful or not. I just wanted to reveal myself entirely as the woman, the human being I have discovered in the full extent of my intellectual and spiritual maturity. *Primera Fila* is both a CD and a DVD that includes a documentary about my evolution and what has led me to become the person I am today. It has been the most important and exciting artistic challenge of my career: to dare to go onstage with almost no makeup, hair tied back, a pair of old jeans—the same pair I wear to sit on the floor and play with my daughter—and the tennis shoes I have had since I was eighteen. Being completely open and honest allowed me to focus entirely on the essence of each song, my voice projecting the thrill of every story, without the distraction of the dancers, the confetti and the special effects.

It was a new way of connecting with my audience. The project was more relaxed than any other project I have done before, and it made me open up and make myself vulnerable. This catharsis was so honest and so positive that in the eyes of my fans it has been one of the most successful albums of my career. The project was a refreshing change for me, opening up endless possibilities, one of which is the book you are holding in your hands, which allowed me to discover the pleasure of sharing things on paper, and the hope that they can turn into positive ideas for whoever reads them.

Daring to Dream

Everyone has a gift, but many people fail to see theirs because of the circumstances they find themselves in. No one was created to feel trapped, depressed or empty. When those feelings cross my mind I have learned to ask myself, What is the purpose of what I am going through? Because everything has a purpose; everything I experience is part of a whole. If I hadn't experienced the death of my loved ones, if I hadn't experienced pain as a little girl, if I hadn't tasted the madness of success, the solitude of fame, its glory and its delusion, if I hadn't cried for love, for the pain of not being able to get pregnant, for a devastating illness like Lyme disease, if I hadn't hit rock bottom, if I hadn't come crashing down . . . I would never have been able to see the great human potential that lies within me.

If I hadn't been through everything I've been through, I would never have discovered the loving, practical, curious, persevering and dedicated person I am today. There are people who are a part of life and there are people who are life itself, and I always work to be a part of that second group. I want to *be* life, energy, strength, drive, power, spirit, courage. . . . I want to be all this with every atom of my being.

God has always been a constant in my life. With Him by my side, I am a survivor, happy and filled with hope. I exist in constant change; my life is in constant evolution. I have the power to decide what I want out of life, how far I want to go and what I want to accomplish. I am filled with desires and needs, but often-times they have nothing to do with the reality of my circum-stances. In such cases it's important for me to recognize who I really am and how far I can go without trespassing on somebody else's freedom. I need to know not to take someone else's com-ments or attitude personally just because that person is coming from a place of pain and insecurity. So I don't take it personally. Nothing is personal.

The moments of separation, mourning, illness and leaving home to move to a new country are the pillars of my existence. These experiences have made me stronger and wiser. These expe-riences have made me who I am. I feel like I have lived many lives, but they have all come together to make me the happy, complete, content and strong person I am today.

At this moment, as I feel I have started to live again, I have a new life before me; it's like a blank book in which I can write a new story, based on the beginning of a new table of contents listing chapters filled with enthusiasm and exciting projects. Among the many projects that await, I plan to continue my love affair with music, discovering new songs that will come to life on the lips of so many magnificent people who have accompanied me throughout my journey. I plan to fall in love with the character or the story that will take me back to the magical world of acting. In that table of contents I can also see numerous projects that will allow me to develop my creativity, my pleasure in sharing life with others, be it through a business project or a new book or another adventure that I can't even imagine. Personally, I want to continue to enjoy the unique gift of a healthy life, and I want to continue to conquer new horizons, such as crossing the Grand Canyon by foot, climbing some of the tallest mountains or setting sail on a boat toward the horizon of happiness. I want to continue to grow every day along with my family, discovering one another, loving one another, caring for one another. I want to establish new friendships, meet interesting people I can learn from and see life from a different perspective. I want to discover new hobbies, such as photography, painting and sculpture, and to continue uncovering new gifts hidden within me.

Each life has its own story, and I am sure that even the hardest moments of my life have had a clear purpose. They may be painful, but I am convinced that everything is possible, because we are transcendent and magnificent beings, equipped with great gifts, if we only look for them. I have learned that when I fall, I must rise and shake the dust from my clothes in order to move on. I am a free human being, a part of the whole. I have a purpose in this world, and with that purpose I will be able to fill everyone around me with light. All of us on this earth are called upon to be life itself!

Today I feel that my existence is filled with light, freedom, accomplishment, and my soul overflows with eternity.

Within me is my present, my today . . . my moment.

Nothing and nobody can take this away from me as I live life, *growing stronger* with every passing day.

· EPILOGUE ·

I never thought of or imagined an epilogue for this book, much less one of this nature. But life is always full of unexpected situations and surprises, and here I find myself trying to see the positive side of this new life lesson.

The morning of May 27, 2011, I woke up to a peculiar silence in my home; usually my daughter Sabrina's little songs and giggles wake me up each day. I got dressed and went downstairs to the kitchen, intrigued by the aura that seemed to consume my home. I didn't know what was going on, and Tommy had already taken care of everything so that Sabrina would be in the park with her friends. I was surprised to find my doctor standing in the living room, and I walked over to him, asking, "What are you doing here? Come, sit down. . . . What can I get you? Would you like a cup of coffee?" That was when Tommy came walking toward me quickly, with an unusual expression on his face.

"Baby, come. . . . Sit with me in the living room."

I felt something instantly, and immediately asked, "What happened?"

"Baby, your sister Fede called me. . . . Your mother fell. . . ."

In that moment I felt that my heart was going to burst through my mouth, and my stomach shrank.

"What happened?" The words came out like a pleading scream. "Tell me what happened."

"Baby, your mother has passed away."

Those words just lingered in the air as I ran around the room in complete hysterics.

"No, no, no, no . . . it's a lie. It can't be true." I ran to the phone and called her house to ascertain it, hoping to hear her voice, but on the other end of the line I heard the cries of my sisters, confirming what had happened, and giving way to the greatest nightmare that I have ever imagined possible.

I screamed, I ran, I knelt . . . I cried in despair . . . I pleaded— while everyone in my house embraced me and cried with me, and my doctor even forced me to take a sedative with the hopes of calming me down, so that my emotions wouldn't affect the baby I was slated to deliver in just three or four weeks. My mother had left my house just a few days ago and would never again return . . . ever.

At that moment began the greatest of all my life lessons, sent just then by God. Hours upon interminable hours passed from the time that I received the news until I reached Mexico City to be by my mother's side. From the moment I took off in New York, the trip felt claustrophobic and eternal, coupled with the fact that we left the airport and drove directly to the funeral, adding even more interminable minutes to the ordeal—since the cars and vans of the press surrounded the car where my husband and I were. They wanted to take as many photos as possible, forcing us to drive at a speed of ten kilometers per hour, when I wanted to fly so that I could finally be by my mother's side.

Even as I arrived, I had the hope that the whole thing would be a lie, a bad dream, but when I discovered my sisters crying in front of my mother's coffin, my knees buckled and I felt the certainty of this harrowing new reality.

It was true. . . . My mother had passed away.

My sisters and I hugged one another with the force that comes only with the most intense pain, all of us becoming one in that moment of insurmountable agony.

We looked one another in the eyes and kept saying, "My sister . . . sister . . . my sister . . . my mother. . . ."

That was the onset of a critical lesson that we could have learned only that way. We were now united by the even stronger bond of our sisterhood, despite our differences and different ways of thinking, but with the feeling that we were all there for one another, for the first time, from a place of total sincerity and the deepest of love.

We watched over our mother for hours, each of us with our family, saying good-bye to her in accordance with our personal beliefs and needs for expression in such moments.

Since my mother had already accepted God into her heart and was baptized under the Christian faith, my sister, accompanied by her church's orchestra, sang hymns praising God, thanking Him for His love, greatness and wisdom.

My sister Laura offered a Catholic Mass.

My sister Ernestina chose to comply with my mother's last wish: "Honey, Mauricio," my mother said to Titi and to Titi's future husband one day in the past, "things always happen at weddings. Whatever happens, promise me that both of you will push forward." And that is just what they did; they had promised my mother that they would prevail and they did; before all the surviving relatives, amid all our pain, Titi and Mauricio were married. We all supported her decision, knowing that love had triumphed over death. Titi said to me, "Thalita, today my mother was going to see me dressed in white for my wedding, and I turned out to be the one who had to see her dressed in white for her union with God."

And at the end, I asked for a group of mariachis, dressed in white and gold, to sing the songs that my mother loved best, with their music shattering the intensity of that moment.

My mother always got what she wanted, and this was no exception, since on countless occasions she told Titi to send a wedding invitation to her sister Laura, to unite the family. And she would tell me to attend Titi's wedding, to which I would respond that, as per my doctor's orders, as I was just weeks away from my delivery, it would be virtually impossible.

Regardless, there we all were, my sister Laura at Titi's wedding, and me—putting all risk aside—signing as a witness. All of this took place in front of my mother, who I am sure would have been overjoyed to see us all together as she had so yearned.

Just days prior to her death her words had been like an omen; Fidel, who had worked in my mother's house for over fourteen years, went to pick my mother up from the airport after she had visited me, and told me that she said something to him. "Fidelito, I arrived for Titinita's wedding, and I will be back to New York on Tuesday." And that was just what happened. Her body was transported in its coffin to New York, but the paperwork was not finalized because it was a holiday weekend, so it had to be sent out on a different flight. The airline that transported her changed everything around and arranged it so that my mother would not have to wait in the airport one more day. Her remains traveled on Tuesday, and that was how she arrived to this city, exactly as she planned it. On top of that she arrived during Memorial Day weekend, on Veterans Day, a day when we commemorate the life and work of the great war veterans—which was perfectly poignant, because she was the ultimate trouper.

And without her knowing it, with her insightful words, even at her final hours, she foretold what was going to happen.

Gude, who had also spent many years working for my mother, heard her say: "Gude, don't wake me up tomorrow; tomorrow is my day of rest—tomorrow all day is for rest."

Our mother had one final wish, and to grant it we would have to travel to New York. Many times she said that if she were to die, she wanted to be brought to this part of the United States, where she could enjoy the different seasons. She loved the flowers, the air, the leaves as they changed colors, the pollen drifting in the breeze, the birds . . . the albino squirrels and beloved deer.

All of us traveled to be with her: my grandmother, my sisters—Laura, her firstborn, Federica, Gabriela, Ernestina—and me, her baby, and on behalf of all her grandchildren: Quetzalcoatl Xavier, her first grandson, and Tedoro.

She arrived at the place where she wanted to be, where she belonged, from where she came, with a Christian ceremony that I delivered, accompanied by a string duet that interpreted Bach, Vivaldi and Mozart pieces—the whole gathering covered in white roses, which she loved so much.

That was how we said good-bye to our mother, with unity through pain, enveloped in love—a sisterly love that has always been there, and that emerged then with such force that it made us one, while still preserving our individuality, like the fingers of one hand, which are each independent and different but, united by the palm, become indissoluble and inseparable, always feeling the innate power of a closed fist.

Just as we know that we will never again see her on this plane, that we will no longer feel the warmth of her hands or hear her voice, her laugh, her advice, her jokes, or feel her immense desire to live with the intensity of every hurricane, every sea, every land and every forest—that's also how we know we will find her; we will see her again, and we will know why her unexpected loss left us yearning for her spirit.

In moments like these, it seems that God creates our lives in such unexpected ways, and some people might find themselves angry with Him, demanding to know why, and claiming, "God, I don't get Your sense of humor," or "I don't understand Your message or Your teachings. . . . What is it that I have to learn?" In my case, after speaking to Him like this, I had a flash of understanding when I realized what His plan really was. I understood, from another perspective, outside my pain, that He, knowing the day that each one of us is going to die, had already designed a perfect plan. He placed a life inside me so that it would give me strength to not die myself, given the immense love that I have for my mother; He placed a man in Titi's path so that she would be taken care of; next to Laura, He put a man full of optimism, with whom she worked intensely on her recovery and spiritual growth; and He made Fede a part of her tremendous love and presence, assuring her she would always know with full faith that my mother was called to the presence of God, and that one day we would see her again. And the one who got the best birthday present was Gabi—a beautiful breakfast celebration from my mother . . . the last birthday that she spent with one of her daughters.

Somebody who is well remembered never dies. My mother

lives in the sky, but she also lives here with us through our memories and stories about her, told by all those who knew and loved her. She will live on through me, through my family, through her grandchildren and great-grandchildren, through her friends; we will foster the memory of her life that celebrates it by always remembering her anecdotes, her great moments, those afternoons of laughter, her brilliance, her steadiness, her sense of humor, her vitality and force in getting up each and every time to face any adversity, always graceful, triumphant and stronger every day.

This example of a life, like so many that have come before us, can serve to ground us on a new path that lets us fully enjoy the simplest things and the people who, in the simple act of being around every day, allow us to forget how quickly life can change, given that life is so fragile and can easily escape with one breath.

We should love intensely, without being afraid to say it, without limitations—if you want, show your love in the form of an embrace. Just do it! Don't linger in a state of longing; if you want to kiss someone, just go for it. Let your feelings flow; if you want to look into the eyes of this other person forever, look into them; speak without words through your heart. Allow yourself to stop and smell the flowers; close your eyes and feel the warmth of the sun in every pore of your skin; run beneath the rain, laugh and enjoy every instant; and don't get worked up about things that you will later realize weren't worth it.

If you harbor any pain in your heart, any resentment, free yourself through forgiveness. The pressure and all of that accumulated pain just are not worth it, because at the end of the day we don't know how much time we have left to make amends and live in peace; we don't know when the clock of our life stops. The only one who knows is God, so be free; be yourself; be brave enough not to have remorse about *anything*; live life fully; enjoy your loved ones as if it is the last day you are ever going to see them; don't leave anything for tomorrow, because we never know whether tomorrow will come; do something surprising and spontaneous every day; leave blame in the past; start to build a foundation of love by living one day at a time; and most of all, take the hand of God and enjoy the magnitude of His potential in this great adventure we call *life!*

·   ACKNOWLEDGMENTS   ·

To my two families: my blood family, with whom I was born—to my mother, who has always been and will always be by my side in this life, and to my sisters, their children and our grandmother, with whom I share the joy of life—and the family that I chose with all of my love and consciousness.

To my Tommy, who has been my fundamental pillar in every circumstance that I have faced since the moment that I decided to walk with him.

To my daughter, Sabrina, who each day reminds me of something forgotten from my own youth, and whose smile illuminates every day of my life.

To my precious son Matthew, you are in my arms giving me a new reason to always fight to actualize my dreams.

To my extended family, my fans, who have stayed with me through every facet of my transitions and search, and who have always been loving, passionate and so attentive to me as a person.

To my father, who, despite not being around for the highlights of my life, implanted in me a fascination for seeking and questioning, and the importance of growing in every aspect of life, be it personal or professional.

To Federica Sodi, my sister, for helping me to find a fresh and fun path for this book. Bob! From the other side of the mountain . . . your Sam!

To Raymond Garcia, for understanding my vision and wanting to relate it to the world in an inspirational and accessible way, and to Kim Suarez, Tracy Bernstein and the whole team of "Penguins" who worked so tirelessly on this book.

To Andrea, for her clinical eye that helped me improve and enhance every detail, every story and every idea.

To Maria Cristina, for those excellent conversations, and for daring to mount a trapeze, just to put herself in my shoes.

To everyone who helped get this book into the hands of my readers.

And to many of those whose words have been influential in my life: Joel Osteen, for inviting us to his table; Alice Miller, for resolving my "drama of the child who was doted upon"; Beatriz Sheridan, for giving me the strength to understand my own potential; Edmund J. Bourne, for writing *The Anxiety & Phobia Workbook,* my invaluable work tool; Dr. Horowitz and Dr. Patricia Volkow for their extensive knowledge on the subject of Lyme's disease; Sri Swami Sivananda for his insights and practice; Arthur Schopenhauer for giving meaning to my most hidden thoughts.

To my God, for being the axis around which I orbit—that attraction, that sense of gravity that attracts me to His strength and magnitude. Like the planets orbit around the sun, and without it would move along with no direction, lost in the vastness of the universe, so, too, my God shines to illuminate and warm each day, to revitalize and nurture my heart and soul.

B T365
ThalGia.
Growing stronger /

FLORES
03/12

HFLOW